BOOK OF
INDIAN LIFE CRAFTS

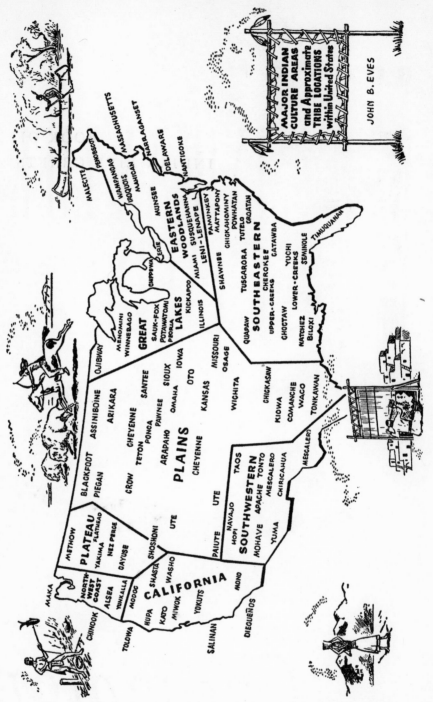

MAJOR INDIAN CULTURE AREAS and Approximate TRIBE LOCATIONS within United States

JOHN B. EVES

EASTERN WOODLANDS

MALECITE
PENOBSCOT
WAMPANOAG
IROQUOIS
MAHICAN
MASSACHUSETTS
NARRAGANSET
MUNSEE
DELAWARE
NANTICOKE
ERIE
CHIPPEWA
MIAMI
LENI - LENAPE
SUSQUEHANNA
SHAWNEE
PAMUNKEY
MATTAPONY
CHICKAHOMINY
POWHATAN
TUTELO
CROATAN
CATAWBA
TUSCARORA
CHEROKEE
YUCHI
SEMINOLE
TIMUQUANAN

SOUTHEASTERN

QUAPAW
UPPER - CREEKS
LOWER - CREEKS
CHOCTAW
NATCHEZ
BILOXI

GREAT LAKES

OJIBWAY
MENOMINI
WINNEBAGO
SAUK-FOX
POTAWATOMI
PEORIA
KICKAPOO
ILLINOIS

PLAINS

ASSINIBOINE
ARIKARA
BLACKFOOT
PIEGAN
CROW
CHEYENNE
TETON
SANTEE
PAWNEE
PONCA
OMAHA
IOWA
SIOUX
OTO
MISSOURI
OSAGE
KANSAS
ARAPAHO
CHEYENNE
WICHITA
CHICKASAW
COMANCHE
WACO
KIOWA
TONKAWAN

PLATEAU

METHOW
YAKIMA
FLATHEAD
NEZ PERCE
CAYUSE
SHOSHONI
UTE

SOUTHWESTERN

UTE
PAIUTE
TAOS
NAVAJO
HOPI
APACHE
TONTO
MESCALERO
CHIRICAHUA
MESCALERO
MOHAVE
YUMA

NORTH WEST COAST

MAKA
CHINOOK
ALSEA
YUNKALLA
MODOC

CALIFORNIA

SHASTA
WASHO
HUPA
KATO
MIWOK
YOKUTS
MONO
SALINAN
DIEGUEÑOS
TOLOWA

BOOK OF

INDIAN LIFE CRAFTS

By OSCAR E. NORBECK

Illustrated by JOHN B. EVES

ASSOCIATION PRESS · NEW YORK

Book of Indian Life Crafts

Association Press, 291 Broadway, New York 7, N. Y.

Second Printing

Library of Congress catalog card number: 58-5037

55

Printed in the United States of America
By American Book–Stratford Press, Inc., New York

To Ann

"To those who know thee not,
No words can paint!
And those who know thee,
Know all words are faint!"

—Hanna More

NAVAHO PRAYER

In beauty may I walk;
With beauty before me, may I walk;
With beauty behind me, may I walk;
With beauty above me, may I walk;
With beauty below me, may I walk;
With beauty all around me, may I walk;
In beauty, may my walk be finished;
In beauty, may my walk be finished.

TABLE OF CONTENTS

ACKNOWLEDGMENTS

This work has been compiled from examination of many collections, personal observations and study of photographs and prints. In many instances, book references to the subject are so slight and scattered that no reference list is given at the end of some projects.

The reader must realize that some statements in this book must have a broad and general concept, and that exceptions are bountiful in Indian lore.

The author and publisher of *Book of Indian Life Crafts* have undertaken to give credit and secure permissions from copyright holders of material reprinted. In a few cases, it was not possible to determine original sources or to locate publishers. Upon notification of the omission of any proper credit, the publisher of this book will gladly make corrections in future editions.

We wish to express our deep appreciation to all who helped make this work possible. We are particularly indebted to Dr. Dorothy Cross, New Jersey State Museum Anthropological Adviser, for her many practical suggestions and corrections.

To all the kind, patient, and helpful folks in the Trenton, N. J. Public Library.

To the dedicated folks in the Department of Indian Art, Denver

Art Museum, who have developed the *Indian Leaflet Series*, which has been our constant guide and quite often the "final word" in this work.

To the Executive Secretary of the Chicago, Ill. Indian Council Fire, Marion Gridley, whose *Indians of Yesterday* and other works on Indian Life, has been a steadying influence in our efforts to capture the interest and imagination of boys and girls.

To Wayne Replogle, whose *Yellowstone's Bannock Trails* was a constant source of encouragement for this part-time writer.

To Robert Bunker, author of *Other Men's Skies*, who, perhaps more than any other contemporary writer, has opened the door for us into the very heart and mind of the North American Indian.

To Roland Burdick, Association Press Promotion Manager and Editorial Associate, who persuaded us to do something with our seventeen year collection of Indian notes. We know of no man who wears the robe of patience with more aplomb and graciousness.

To Martharie Michael, for her many hours of patiently deciphering our writing, and transforming it into clean copy for the publisher.

To John Eves for his sterling art work, ability to read our mind and make this work come to life.

Our heartfelt thanks to Jane Eves for cheerfully checking all art copy and keying in the illustrations.

And finally, an affectionate and reverent bow to "my severest critic and best friend," my wife, Ann, who possesses the uncanny power of making our most obstinate bits of writing become ridiculously obvious and simple.

O. E. Norbeck

Winder Village, Bristol, Pennsylvania

INTRODUCTION

Perhaps the best way to get the most out of this book would be for the reader first to discover the wide scope of units and individual projects as outlined in the Table of Contents and Index. Then set up a definite program, unit by unit, especially if the reader is a group leader or instructor, keeping in mind a well-balanced program for a small group, department or camp-wide effort. Many of the projects lend themselves well for a combination effort of fathers and sons or mothers and daughters.

The reader will find detailed, step by step procedures for each project, with illustrations conceived and executed by the artist, John Eves, who combines a rare appreciation and understanding of Indian life and crafts with masterful strokes of the pen and brush.

We have tried to anticipate the Indian craft questions of boys, girls, adults, agency leaders and instructors, camp counselors, and teachers and all the projects in the book have been tested by craft instructors, teachers, fathers and sons in the YMCA Father-Son Indian Guides movement, the author and the illustrator.

We sincerely hope that the reader will take time to read the introductory notes for each project and unit, before beginning actual construction. Telling your admiring friends *how* and *why* your finished product was used by the Indians will add much to your personal pride and satisfaction and enlighten your listener.

We have built on the premise that many phases of Indian life, arts and crafts, which we now consider purely recreational, were completely utilitarian and functional for the Indian. The author and illustrator have tried to develop this book, step by step, out of the daily lives of the Indian, from individual to tribe, his manner of dress, his arts and crafts, his dwellings, communications, transportation, ceremonial equipment, food, cooking, implements and utensils, pottery, weaving, toys, furniture, games and sports.

The early white settlers were forced by circumstances to incorporate Indian knowledge into their daily lives for the sake of survival and much that we have learned from the Indian has become so firmly embedded in our American life that it is impossible at times to recognize its true origin.

Animal flesh and fish, the wild fruits, roots, and berries, the cultivation of vegetables nourished the Indian; skins sheltered and clad him; wood, stone, and bone armed and equipped him. The early Indian had no knowledge of metals, but he used a stone hammer and war club; he chipped flint knives and arrowpoints, tanned skins, baked pots, and invented the bow and arrow.

He had a hunting companion, the dog, which was also his beast of burden and to him, the very sun, moon, and the stars were persons; the animals, trees, and mountains were great powers.

The Indian enjoyed sharing and borrowing, and to a great extent, their habit has become an unconscious process in the American way of life.

From the Atlantic to the Pacific, the Indian has hunted, farmed, played, and fought. Although they were all Indians, they were divided into many tribes, each tribe having different language, different style homes, different costumes, and different ways of living.

Our curiosity and imagination has been captured by the customs, arts, and crafts of the Indian. We watch, and try to imitate their dances; we buy, and try to make their jewelry, costumes, pottery, musical instruments, and blankets; we are fascinated by their symbols, designs and motifs; we become interested in their methods of communication and transportation. In short, their way of life and master craftsmenship has captured the imagination and interest of young and old, and has swelled the growing ranks of Indian lore enthusiasts. Today we draw on their rich heritage and knowledge in creating an interesting and satisfying hobby.

BOOK OF
INDIAN LIFE CRAFTS

1. COSTUME

INDIAN WEARING APPAREL

CLASSIFYING Indian wearing apparel and ornaments into cultural and regional areas is a well-nigh exhausting experience in research. We must sift our information from many sources and areas. We must study details that were common to most Indians of a general region, rather than purely local patterns.

In our chapter on costumes and ornaments we have endeavored to combine the surviving fragments of a long extinct way of life, patiently sifting the many rapid changes that took place with the coming of the white man. We must also recognize that Indians loved to trade and exchange tribal costumes, ornaments, and ceremonial equipment. The Indian was always on the look-out for a new style. Jackets, shirts, and vests appeared early in Colonial times, and the Indian was quick to adopt the apparel of the white man. The arrival of the white man created a modification and change in costumes over a vast area of Indian country.

Tanned skin of the deer family was generally the material for clothing throughout the greater part of the country. The hide of the buffalo was worn for robes by tribes of the plains and even for dresses and leggings by older people. Fabrics of bark, hair, mountain sheep wool, and feathers were made in the North Pacific, Pueblo land, and southern regions, and cotton has been woven by the Hopi from ancient times. Sinew from the tendons of the larger animals was the usual sewing material, but fibers of plants was also employed. Sewing was practiced by both sexes, and each sex usually made its own clothing.

The stereotype costume of the Indian man was tanned buckskin, and consisted of a shirt, breechcloth, leggings tied to a belt or waist strap, and moccasins.

The shirt, which hung free over the hips, was provided with crude sleeves and was designed to be drawn over the head.

The woman's costume differed from that of the man in the length of the shirt, which had short sleeves hanging loosely over the upper arm. Women also wore a belt to confine the garment to the waist.

Robes of skin, woven fabrics, and feathers were also worn, but blankets were substituted for these later.

Tribal differences made changes in cut, color, and ornamentation. The edges were often fringed. Quill embroidery and beadwork, painting, scalp-locks, tails of animals, feathers, claws, hoofs, shells, teeth, etc., were applied as ornaments or charms.

Cloth, beads, bells, metals, firearms, steel tools, pipes, and many other articles found their way to the most remote tribes by way of trade and barter.

REFERENCES: *Indian Leaflet Series,* Numbers 89, 90, 91, 92-93, 94-95, 96-97, 108 and 109; Department of Indian Art, Denver Art Museum, 1300 Logan St., Denver, Colorado. Bibliography: American Museum of Natural History, *Costumes of the Plains Indians,* Clark Wissler. Anthropological Papers, 17:2, 1915.

Smithsonian Institution, *American Indian Costumes in the U. S. National Museum*—Herbert A. Krieger, Annual Report for 1928, 1929.

Bureau of American Ethnology, *The Indians of the Southeastern United States*—John R. Swanton. Bulletin 137, 1946. Bulletin 30, pages 310 and 312.

Indian Costume Kits: A full line of costume materials and kits are supplied by a number of trading posts about the country including: Plume Trading & Sales Co., Inc., Box 585, Monroe, New York; Grey Owl Indian Craft Co., 4518 7th Ave. Brooklyn, 20, New York; and Pawnee Bill's Trading Post, Pawnee, Oklahoma.

HEADBANDS

Indian fashions changed just as ours do today; therefore, we cannot say positively just what costumes and ornaments were, or were not, worn at any given period by any one tribe.

Each tribe had its distinctive headgear, which differed in design, color, and detail, according to the purpose for which it was used. Much of the feather work in which American Indians were expert were used as decorations, ornaments, badges of office and honor, proof of bravery, for ceremonials, and as symbols.

Headband: In general, decorated headbands were worn by the southwest New Mexico and Arizona Pueblos, including the Zuni, Acoma, Taos, Navaho, and Apache tribes; the eastern woodland Algonquins and the Delawares of Pennsylvania and New Jersey. The feather headgear of the Forest Indians had no tail, but did circle the head. They stood erect, rather than drooping, as in the Plains.

War Bonnet: It would be wise for the beginner to confine himself to headbands and not attempt a complicated war bonnet. Even a skilled craftsman can save much times and effort by buying and assembling a war bonnet kit, which can be readily found in hobby shops, trading posts, mail order houses, and variety stores.

Indian Materials You Can Use: (band) fur, cloth, leather, leather thong (thong is leather lacing).

Substitute Materials: Felt, suede, ribbon, hat band, oil cloth, cardboard or leather shoe string.

Tools and Equipment You Will Need: Needle, scissors, linen thread No. 15 for cloth and No. 25 for leather. Metal punch for tin can tops.

Indian Decorations: Nuts, seeds, shells, horse hair, rabbit tails, leather thongs, glass or wooden beads, vegetable, berry or root dyes, large and small feathers and fluffs, small bird and animal bones and teeth.

Substitute Decorations: Crayons, colored pencils, oil paints, quick-drying lacquers, water or poster paints, ribbons, colored yarn, jingle bells, elbow macaroni.

Instructions for Making Headband: Headband should not be more than two inches wide. Measure your head size with a strip

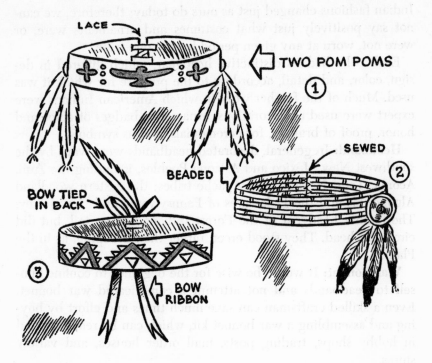

of cardboard or cloth tape measure. Make your choice of materials from the listing.

The Head Plume (Fig. 4) can be made with a piece of leather thong or you can substitute a piece of painted or dyed clothesline. Tie in the back with a simple bow knot.

Pom-poms (Fig. 6) on the sides of the band (above the ears) will add beauty to your headband. The pom-pom can be made with a piece of cardboard, heavy foil, or foil milk tops, or the tops of small frozen fruit cans. First, sew small feathers in a circular formation to the band (Fig. 7) then place the pom-pom directly on top of the circle of feathers and sew it securely to the band, using No. 8 thread.

If you plan to use a metal medallion on the pom-pom, it can be simply attached to the band by punching holes near the center and securing it in the same manner as sewing on a button.

To prevent tearing of the band by the lacing, simply sew button holes where the band is attached at the back of the head.

For details on making beaded band (Fig. 2) see Chapter 2. How to Make Indian Beadwork.

Headband can be fastened simply in the back by tying a bow knot (Fig. 3) or by lacing (Fig. 1). You may prefer to sew it (Fig. 2) together, or use a piece of elastic or snap buttons.

Decorating Your Headband: Refer to the listing of Indian and Substitute Decorations for your decorative materials; then turn to Chapter 4, How to Use Indian Symbols, Designs and Motifs, and pick out your favorite regional tribal designs, and carefully decorate your headband. *Ar. Pg. 102*

Decorate the center of the pom-pom with Indian symbols, using bright colored paints, crayons, colored yarn, etc.

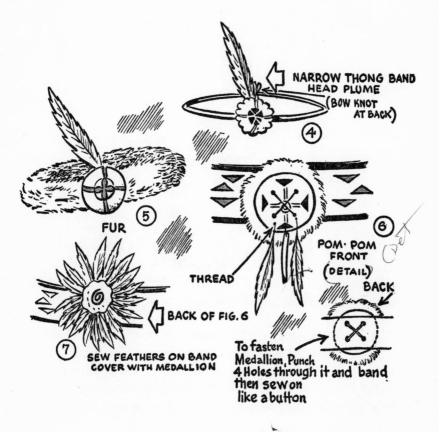

NARROW THONG BAND
HEAD PLUME
(BOW KNOT AT BACK)

④

FUR ⑤

⑥

POM·POM
FRONT
(DETAIL)
BACK

THREAD

BACK OF FIG. 6

⑦ SEW FEATHERS ON BAND
COVER WITH MEDALLION

To fasten
Medallion, Punch
4 Holes through it and band
then sew on
like a button

Elbow macaroni can be painted various colors and sewn on for imitation bone.

If you decide to paint your headband, be sure to allow one color to dry before applying another. Use bright colors. Most important of all—use your imagination!

The American Indians used ornamental bands on their arms, wrists, legs, ankles, and tight-fitting bands around the neck.

They were worn (most by warm climate Indians) during pow-wows, feasts, ceremonials and dances. After the coming of the white man, Indian dancers adopted the use of bells on their ankle bands.

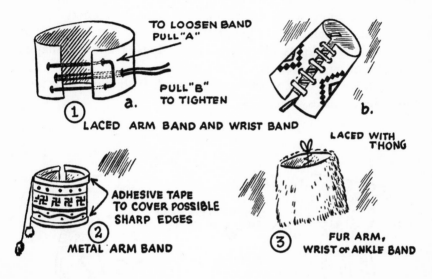

Indian Materials You Can Use: You can make your arm, wrist, leg, ankle, or neck bands out of the same kind of Indian materials as listed for headbands, or you may wish to add Angora goats hair to your ankle bands, or use copper or silver for arm and wrist bands, preferably 18 gauge.

Substitute Materials: Tin, tin cans or aluminum. Substitute white yarn for Angora goats hair.

Tools and Equipment You Will Need: Refer to tools and equipment for headband. In addition, if you plan to work with metal, you will need metal cutting shears (use caution), large nail or nail punch, and small hammer; adhesive tape (half inch) for covering the sharp edgings.

Indian Decorations: See decorations for headbands.

Substitute Decorations: See decorations for headbands.

Instructions for Making Ceremonial Bands: Make your choice of materials from the listing for Headgear. If you prefer to make your arm and wrist bands out of metal (preferably 18 gauge), such as copper, silver, aluminum, tin or tin cans, be careful in cutting it, especially tin; and be sure to cover the sharp edgings with a half inch wide strip of adhesive tape or scotch tape.

The arm bands (Figs. 2, 3, and 6) can be made from one to four inches wide; the gauntlet-type wrist covering (Figs. 4 and 5) can be as long as six inches and also worn for archery.

All bands, including the gauntlet type, can be fastened together by simple bow knots (Fig. 9), lacing (Figs. 1 and 4), snap-on buttons, or metal eyelets.

Fig. 3 is a fur arm, wrist, or ankle band. It should not be more than three inches wide.

④ GAUNTLET TYPE BAND
FITTING SNUGLY AT WRIST

⑤

SHOE LACE or THONG

⑥ BEADED WRIST BAND

BELLS ATTACHED WITH HEAVY THREAD

ANKLE BAND WITH FETLOCK

⑦

STRING

⑩ YARN

⑧ ANKLE BAND WITH BELLS

BOW KNOT NECK BAND

⑨

Fig. 5 shows how to wear the combination arm band and gauntlet-type wrist band.

Fig. 6 is a beaded wrist band with fringe edging. It can also be worn as an arm band as shown in Fig. 5. For detailed beadwork, refer to Chapter 2.

Fig. 7 is a combination ankle bell strap and Angora goats hair fetlock, usually worn by dancers. The ankle bell strap can be worn separately (Fig. 8). A very small dog collar makes an excellent ankle strap. Attach small toy or sleigh bells with heavy thread or punch holes with an awl and tie the bells with thong or shoe strings. Bells can be bought in any toy or baby shop, antique store or trading post.

White yarn makes a good imitation Angora fetlock. See Fig. 10 for detail construction. Use enough material to create fullness.

Most important of all, use the materials at hand, just as the Indians did; and don't forget, use your imagination!

Decorating Your Bands: Refer to Chapter 4, How to Use Indian Symbols, Designs, and Motifs. Choose your favorite or regional tribal designs and carefully decorate your bands. Check the various decorative materials listed under Headbands and Other Bands. Decorate your bands as outlined for the headband. You can add tassels of fur, leather thongs, ribbons, small bird feathers and fluffs, or bits of metal, etc.

And don't forget, instead of painting designs on the metal wrist and arm bands, you can stamp the figures with a large nail or nail punch. And once again, be careful with the metal cutting shears!

The arrival of the white man modified and changed Indian costumes over a large area of America.

The vest, as an Indian garment, appeared early in Colonial times, and is highly favored among the northern Blackfeet, the Chippewas, the Siouxs, and the Crows. It served the Indian as an ornamental garment and a wind-breaker.

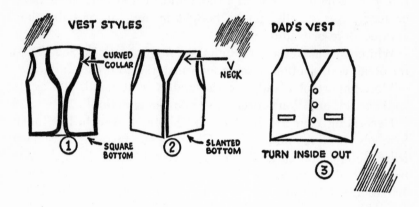

The various styles, Figs. 1, 2, and 3, indicate European origin.

A completely beaded vest was a work of art and highly prized by the owner.

Indian Materials You Can Use: Leather and wool cloth.

Substitute Materials: Felt, denim, burlap, canvas, plastic, ticking, flannel, oil cloth, imitation leather, and double-napped suede.

Tools and Equipment You Will Need: Needle, measuring tape, marking chalk or pencil, wrapping paper or newspaper for pattern, linen thread No. 15 for cloth, and No. 25 for leather, and, if you prefer, a sewing machine.

Indian Decorations: See decorations as listed under Headbands.

Substitute Decorations: See substitute decorations listed under Headbands.

Instructions for Making Vest: First, decide on the kind of material you wish to use for your vest. Then choose the style or cut of your vest from the suggestions in Figs. 1, 2, and 3.

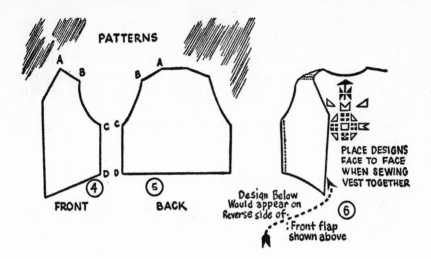

PATTERNS

A
B

A
B

C C

D D

④
FRONT

⑤
BACK

PLACE DESIGNS
FACE TO FACE
WHEN SEWING
VEST TOGETHER

Design Below
Would appear on
Reverse side of

⑥

Front flap
shown above

Trace your pattern on newspaper or wrapping paper, tracing one piece for the back and two pieces for the front, as in Figs. 4 and 5, remembering to add some looseness, and add about one quarter inch for French seams along the sides. A French seam simply means sewing the material on one side, then reversing it and sewing it on the other side. Always remember to sew the first seam of a French seam on the right side of the material.

Pin the pattern together and try on for size. When satisfied, trace your pattern on the material and cut.

Sew back pieces and two front pieces together from A to B and from C to D, as shown in Figs. 4 and 5.

Red or blue flannel, about a half inch wide, makes a good seam binder.

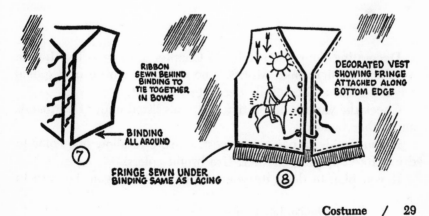

RIBBON
SEWN BEHIND
BINDING TO
TIE TOGETHER
IN BOWS

BINDING
ALL AROUND

⑦

FRINGE SEWN UNDER
BINDING SAME AS LACING

DECORATED VEST
SHOWING FRINGE
ATTACHED ALONG
BOTTOM EDGE

⑧

Use leather thongs for lacing the front (Fig. 7). Brown shoe laces or leather shoe laces can be substituted for thongs.

A good imitation vest can be made out of a discarded suit vest (Fig. 3). Turn it inside out, and cut it to fit your size; bind or hem the edges, using a one and a half inch wide binder of cloth or ribbon.

Fig. 8 shows a cloth or soft leather fringe edging, about three inches wide, which can be sewn to the under-side of the waist line hem or binder.

Only the very advanced bead-worker should attempt a completely beaded vest. See Chapter 2, How to Make Indian Beadwork, for detailed instructions on sewing beads directly to the material.

Front   ⑨   Back

Decorating Your Vest: Refer to Chapter 4, How to Use Indian Symbols, Designs, and Motifs. Choose your favorite or regional tribal designs and carefully decorate your vest.

Check the various decorative materials listed under Headbands and Other Bands.

If you decide to paint your vest, be sure to allow one color to dry before applying another. Use bright colors.

If you plan to decorate your designs with crayon, be sure to iron the backside of the vest to melt the wax, which will eliminate smearing.

You might wish to use cut-out bits of Indian-designed colored cloth or felt and applique (sew) them directly on to the vest.

Fig. 9 shows a V-neck vest with Plains Indian geometric designs. The Woodland Indians used floral designs.

The early American Indian very rarely wore a shirt. However, it became increasingly popular as time passed.

The tanned skin of the deer family was generally the material for clothing in the greater part of this country.

There is no record of North American Indians making a sleeved garment like a coat, except for a few along the Canadian border.

Body coverings were also made of bark and mountain sheep wool. Feathers were used by the Pacific, Pueblo, and southern Indians, and cotton has been woven by the Hopi from early times.

The sewing material was usually made with the sinew from the tendons of the larger animals and plant fibers. Sewing was practiced by both sexes for the most part, and each sex made its own clothing.

The Indian man wore a tanned buckskin shirt which hung free over the hips, had sleeves, and was designed to be drawn over the head.

Tribal differences made changes in cut, color, and ornamentation. The edges were generally fringed.

Some early shirts were very simple, like a poncho (Fig. 4), made of one or two large skins. The early shirts had the legs of the skin dangling at the bottom, and sometimes the sides were left open. Later on, some were cut square at the bottom, with the sides and sleeves sewn in.

Indian Materials You Can Use: Buckskin (tanned deer skin), wool cloth.

Substitute Materials: Blanket material, monks cloth, outing flannel, unbleached muslin, cotton gabardine, and light-weight canvas.

Tools and Equipment You Will Need: Measuring tape, sharp knife or shears, marking pencil or chalk, linen thread No. 25, wax, dry cleaners garment bag, or paper for pattern.

Indian Decorations: Soft leather, leatherette, or plastic for fringe; quill embroidery, beads, tails of animals, feathers, claws, hoofs, shells, horse hair, thongs.

Substitute Decorations: Crayons, oil paints, quick-drying lacquers, bits of bright colored materials, ribbons, jingle bells, strips of commercial imitation beadwork.

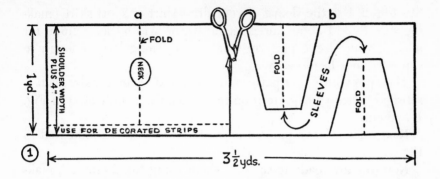

Instructions for Making Indian Shirt: 3½ yards of material will be sufficient for the average-sized boy up to size 18.

We can suggest two ways to make a paper pattern for your Indian shirt. First, simply use your dress shirt or sport shirt as an outline for the front, back, and sleeves, but be sure to mark your pattern about four inches wider on each pattern piece. See Fig. 1. Another simple way to make a pattern is to take a dry cleaners paper garment bag, cut a hole large enough to slip over your head. Check and mark the width of the shoulders for comfort, and cut the length about three inches below your belt line.

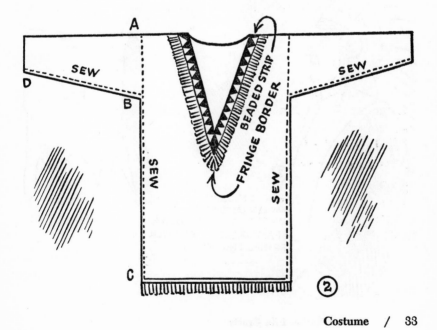

See Fig. 2. Use the sleeve of your dress shirt or sport shirt (making sure to add about three inches to the width) as a guide for making your sleeve pattern. Cut neck opening large enough to slip over your head easily.

Then pin your paper pattern together and try on for size. When satisfied, place your pattern on the materials, as indicated in Fig. 1, and cut.

Next, place sleeve pattern on material and cut as indicated in Fig. 1.

Now you are ready to sew the seams using No. 25 thread, making sure that your material is wrong side out.

Match fold of sleeve with fold of shoulder, as indicated in Fig. 2, and sew from A to B on both sides. Sew bottom of sleeve from D to B, and sew sides of shirt together from B to C.

Hem neck opening and sleeve ends with half-inch colored bias seam tape. Hem bottom of shirt before sewing on fringe. If fringe on bottom of sleeves is desired, you may sew it on after the sleeve is finished, or you may insert it in the seam on the right side of the material before sewing the seam.

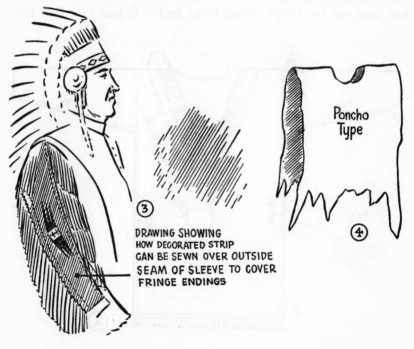

③
DRAWING SHOWING
HOW DECORATED STRIP
CAN BE SEWN OVER OUTSIDE
SEAM OF SLEEVE TO COVER
FRINGE ENDINGS

Poncho
Type

④

Make decorated strips three inches wide and sew on front of shirt to form a triangle, as shown in Fig. 2. Strips can be decorated with beads or paint. If desired, a fringe can be sewn on the underside of the strip before sewing strip on the shirt.

Decorating Your Shirt: Refer to Chapter 4, Indian Arts and Decorations, How to Use Indian Symbols, Designs, and Motifs. Pick out the designs that strike your fancy or were used by the Indians living in your part of the country. Arrange your designs on paper before outlining them on your strips of material.

Some northern and central Indians painted their shirts, and the Plains Indians had long fringes on the shoulders and elbows (Fig. 3). Sometimes they had triangular or square flaps at the front and back. The northern and central shirts had quilled or beaded bands over the shoulders and down the sleeves.

If you decide to decorate with crayons, be sure to iron the reverse side of the material to prevent smearing.

If you are going to use water or poster paint, add some Sanstomerse, Orvarius, or Aerosol, a commercial ingredient which allows the mixture to be applied smoothly and keeps it from rubbing off.

The typical and more familiar costume of the Indian man includes leggings. They are especially evident among the Northern Algonquin-Iroquois, the Southern Seminoles, the Plains with their thigh-leggings, and most of the Southwestern Pueblo, Apache, and Navaho Indians.

Leggings look much like trousers with the seat cut out, similar to the chaps worn by cowboys. They reach from the waist line to the ankles, and are usually held in place by attaching them to the belt with thongs or a belt loop. Sometimes they were attached at the bottom with a strap under the instep, inside the moccasin.

In later years the skin leggings were replaced by red or blue outing flannel or government issued blanket cloth.

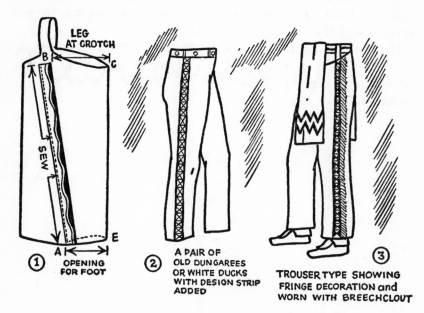

① LEG AT CROTCH — B C SEW A OPENING FOR FOOT E

② A PAIR OF OLD DUNGAREES OR WHITE DUCKS WITH DESIGN STRIP ADDED

③ TROUSER TYPE SHOWING FRINGE DECORATION and WORN WITH BREECHCLOUT

Leggings were not worn all the time. They were worn for warmth in cold weather, on dress occasions, and by hunters as a protection from brush and briers.

Indian Materials You Can Use: Deer or antelope skins, split calfskin or sheepskin.

Substitute Materials: Imitation leather for leggings and fringe, red, blue or brown blanket material, dark blue denim, monks cloth, red or blue outing flannel, or a pair of khaki, denim, duck, or brown trousers. Two strips of two or three inches wide bright colored cloth or ribbon for decorating the sides of the leggings.

Indian Decorations: Vegetable, berry or root dyes, strips of beadwork and leather thongs.

Substitute Decorations: Crayons, colored pencils, water or poster paints, quick-drying lacquers, oil paints, and brushes. Bits of colored cloth or felt to be sewed directly on the leggings.

Tools You Will Need: Wrapping paper or newspaper for pattern, measuring tape, large scissors or shears, pins, marking chalk or crayon, No. 15 thread, and sewing machine.

Instructions for Making Leggings: Make your choice from the three styles, Figs. 1, 2, 3. Fig. 1 is the typical Indian style leggings. Fig. 2 is a pair of blue denim, khaki, white duck, or brown trousers with a decorated strip of material down the outside seams. Fig. 3 is the trouser type with a fringed decoration down the side seams and cut for wearing with breechclout.

Two yards of material, 24 inches wide, is about right for the

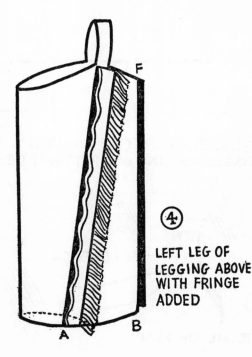

④

LEFT LEG OF
LEGGING ABOVE
WITH FRINGE
ADDED

average sized boy. Before cutting your material, it would be well to make a pattern out of wrapping paper or newspaper, as shown in Fig. 5, by simply folding your pattern paper (1 yard long and 24 inches wide for one legging) lengthwise and cutting out curves B to C, and D to E. Pin paper pattern together, and try on for size. Take your material and cut the length in half; now fold each

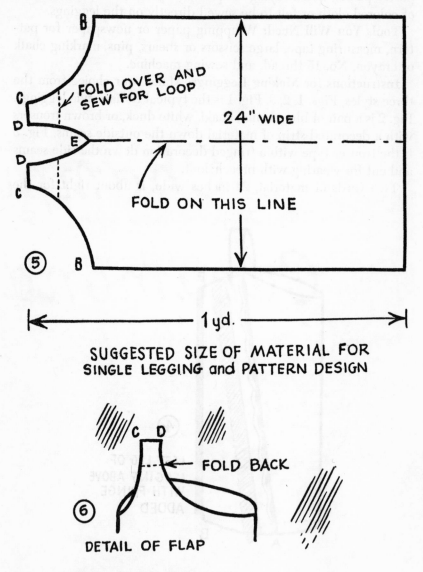

SUGGESTED SIZE OF MATERIAL FOR
SINGLE LEGGING and PATTERN DESIGN

DETAIL OF FLAP

piece lengthwise; then cut the curves B to C and D to E, which permits the leggings to fit under the crotch. Now, pin the goods together (from A to B in Fig. 1) and fit before sewing.

Sew a single seam from A at the bottom center of the legging to B (Fig. 1) a point about the same height as the lower end of the hip pocket on an ordinary pair of trousers.

The upper edge, C-D, should be folded over and sewn down to form a belt loop, as detailed in Fig. 6.

The triangular part of the legging, B-F-A (Fig. 4) is left open like cowboy chaps.

Fig. 4 shows a simple way to add a decorated and fringed strip of soft leather or material to a pair of trousers.

Turn over and bind all edges so that they will not fray or rip.

Decorating Your Leggings: Sew a strip of colored cloth or felt, about 3 inches wide, the entire length of the outside seams on your leggings after they have been decorated.

Refer to Chapter 4, How to Use Indian Symbols, Designs, and Motifs. Choose your favorite or regional tribal designs and carefully decorate the two strips of material. If you paint your designs, be sure to allow one color to dry before applying another. Use bright colors.

If you plan to decorate with crayons, be sure to iron the backside of the material to melt the wax, which will prevent smearing.

Perhaps you prefer to use cut-out bits of Indian-designed colored cloth or felt and applique (sew) them directly to the material.

Or perhaps you might prefer to sew a simple fringe in place of the decorated strip of material.

BREECHCLOTH

Climate and environment determined the materials and style of clothing of the Indian. In prehistoric America, the breechclout (now commonly known as the breechcloth) was practically universal for men and for the most part, women also. The old settlers used to call the breechcloth "Indian breeches." In early times it was made of soft tanned skin, but later on government-issued blanket cloth was used. The breechcloth was usually from four to six feet long and about a foot wide. It passed between the legs and tucked under the belt in front and back. The ends hung down from the belt like narrow aprons and were often decorated. Extra long breechcloths, sometimes reaching to the ankle or touching the ground and elaborately decorated, were used for ceremonials and special occasions.

All Plains Indians used the breechcloth but the Woodland Indians preferred a simple apron. See Figs. 4 and 5.

Indian Materials You Can Use: Doeskin, buffalo hide, duffel cloth, red or blue outing flannel cloth or red or blue blanket cloth.

Substitute Materials: Burlap, denim, wool felt, plastic, lightweight canvas, suede, imitation leather, broadcloth, monks cloth, velveteen, etc.

Tools and Equipment You Will Need: Scissors, needle, linen thread No. 15 for cloth and No. 25 for leather, or sewing machine, yard stick or measuring tape.

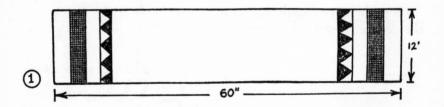

Indian **Decorations:** Vegetable, berry or root dyes, strips of beadwork.

Substitute Decorations: Crayons, colored pencils, oil paints, water or poster paints, colored yarn, or bits of Indian designed colored felt or cloth for applique work. "Applique" simply means to sew the bits of colored cloth directly to the breechcloth.

Instructions for Making Breechcloth: The material for an average-sized boy should be about six feet long and one foot wide, as shown in Fig. 1. Decide your own length by first measuring the total length by passing a measuring tape between your legs and tucking it under your belt in front and back. It should hang down about one inch above your knee caps with the same length in the back.

If you prefer, trim the bottom edges with a fringe effect, cutting narrow strips about three inches long. See Fig. 4.

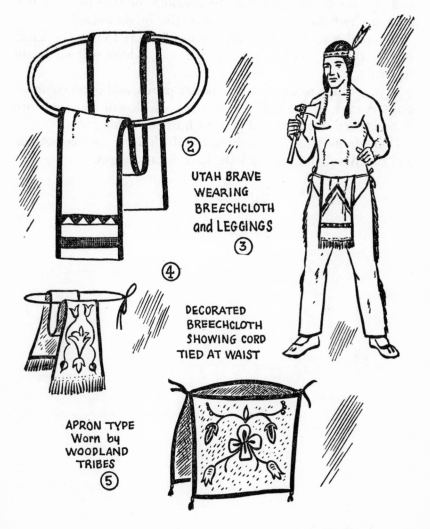

②

UTAH BRAVE WEARING BREECHCLOTH and LEGGINGS ③

④ DECORATED BREECHCLOTH SHOWING CORD TIED AT WAIST

APRON TYPE Worn by WOODLAND TRIBES ⑤

Trim the edges by sewing a one or two inch wide binder out of bias tape or bright colored cloth or ribbon.

Fig. 2 shows how it is worn and Fig. 3 shows a breechcloth worn with a pair of leggings or pants.

Instructions for Decorating Your Breechcloth: See Indian and Substitute Decorations for your decorative materials, then turn to Chapter 4, How to Use Indian Symbols, Designs, and Motifs, and pick out your favorite regional tribal designs, and carefully decorate your breechcloth.

If you decide to paint your breechcloth, be sure to allow one color to dry before applying another. Use bright colors!

If you plan to decorate with crayons, be sure to iron the backside of the breechcloth to melt the wax, which will eliminate smearing.

If you decide to use water or poster paints, add some commercial Orvarius, Sanstomerse, or Aerosol, which will allow mixture to be applied smoothly and prevent it from brushing off.

Don't forget that Plains breechcloth designs are geometrical and the Woodland breechcloths have floral designs.

Indian robes were made of large hides or pelts of small animals sewed together. Sometimes the Indians would cut bird and rabbit skins into ribbons, which were twisted or woven into a robe. The Plains Indians usually wore a robe made of a whole buffalo skin. The robe was usually put on in any way that suited the wearer. Sometimes they were decorated on the flesh side with painted designs, quill or beaded embroidery. The buffalo robe was eventually replaced by government issued blanket cloth and traders wool blankets.

HOW BLANKET ROBE IS WORN

Indian blankets were woven the same as baskets from wool, hair, feathers, down, bark, cotton, etc. They were worn as protection from the weather, during ceremonies, used for bed coverings, hangings, partitions, ownings, and sun shades. They were often decorated with strips of fur, fringes, tassels, pendants, beadwork, and feathers.

With the coming of the white man and as furs became scarce, blankets were in great demand for articles of trade. In 1831 Buffalo, New York, became the manufacturing center of the Mackinaw blanket.

Tribes who were unwilling to adopt the white man's dress were called "blanket Indians." In Taos, New Mexico, half the population, called summer people, are almost always wrapped in a white sheet, while the other half, called the winter people, wear bright red flannel blankets in the winter and light weight cotton blankets in the summer.

With the coming of the Spaniards, the Pueblo tribes received sheep and looms from the conquerors, which created the famous "Navaho Blanket." The Navahos wove blankets with broad bars of white and black called "Chief's pattern," which were worn by the tribal leaders.

It was the custom of the Hopi bridegroom to weave his bride a white cotton blanket, and at her death, wrapped her body in it for the last rites.

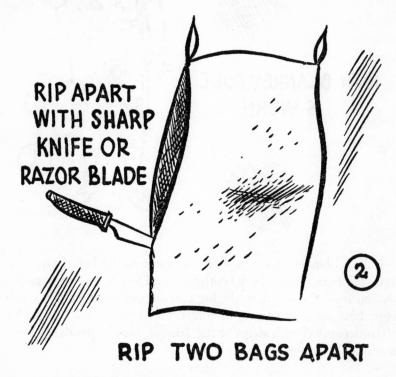

RIP APART
WITH SHARP
KNIFE OR
RAZOR BLADE

②

RIP TWO BAGS APART

Indian Materials You Can Use: A single skin of moose, deer, bear, or buffalo; pelts of fox, beaver, otter, raccoon, squirrel; or handwoven blanket material; wild turkey feathers.

Substitute Materials: Store burlap or burlap sacks, heavy muslin, light-weight canvas, one-color store blanket or monks cloth.

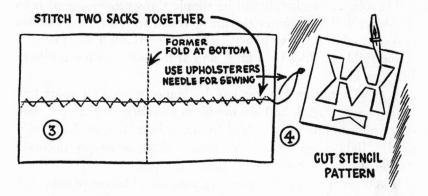

STITCH TWO SACKS TOGETHER

FORMER FOLD AT BOTTOM

USE UPHOLSTERERS NEEDLE FOR SEWING

③

④

CUT STENCIL PATTERN

Tools and Equipment You Will Need: Scissors, large needle (an upholsterer's needle is fine), No. 25 thread, heavy cardboard for stencil, stencil brush, paint brushes, marking chalk, sewing machine, or a large loom, if you plan to weave your own robe or blanket.

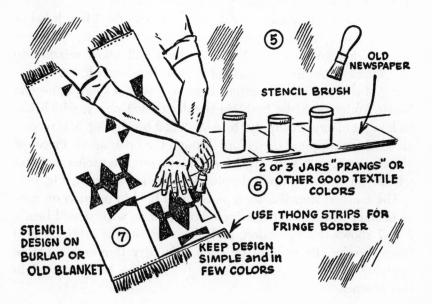

⑤

OLD NEWSPAPER

STENCIL BRUSH

2 or 3 JARS "PRANGS" OR OTHER GOOD TEXTILE COLORS

⑥

USE THONG STRIPS FOR FRINGE BORDER

STENCIL DESIGN ON BURLAP OR OLD BLANKET

⑦

KEEP DESIGN SIMPLE and in FEW COLORS

Indian Decorations: Vegetable, berry or root dyes, horse hair, leather thong, beads, shells, teeth, claws, quills, etc.

Substitute Decorations: Crayons, colored pencils, water or poster paints, or quick-drying lacquers.

Instructions for Making Robe or Blanket: If you plan to wear a skin robe or blanket, it can be simply thrown over one or both shoulders and held under the arms. When traveling, the Indians also secured it at the waist with a belt. Sometimes it was fastened at the right shoulder by a knot, and at the waist with a girdle or belt. See Fig. 1.

A good imitation blanket can be made by ripping apart two burlap sacks, Fig. 2, and sewing them together, as in Fig. 3. You may prefer to buy two yards of brown or blue store burlap, heavy muslin, light-weight canvas or monks cloth, or simply decorate a one-color store blanket with Indian designs.

If you are interested in weaving your own blanket or robe, see Chapter 4, Indian Weaving.

Decorating Your Robe or Blanket: Refer to the listing of Indian and Substitute Decorations for your choice of decorative materials; then turn to Chapter 4, How to use Indian Symbols, Designs, and Motifs, and pick out your favorite regional tribal designs, and carefully decorate your robe or blanket.

If you decide to paint your designs, you can do it free hand or you can use a stencil. In using water or poster paints, add some Ovarius, Sanstomerse, or Aerosol, which will allow mixture to be applied smoothly and prevent it from brushing off.

Fig. 4 shows a stencil pattern being cut with a sharp knife (an X-acto knife would be best) in regular stencil paper, which can be bought in any art supply store. A stencil brush, Fig. 5, is recommended for stippling the colors through the open areas. Pieces of old newspaper are very good for daubing out the excess pigment which you may pick up in dipping into the jars of color, Fig. 6.

The finished stencil is then placed and held in position on robe or blanket while design is stippled onto fabric with stencil brush. Fig. 7 shows this operation, and also suggests the addition of a fringe border. Be sure to let each color dry thoroughly before applying another. Small Indian rugs may also be decorated in this manner.

If you plan to decorate with crayons, be sure to iron the back-side of the material to melt the wax, which will prevent smearing.

REFERENCES: *Bureau of American Ethnology*, Bull. 30, p. 153, Smithsonian Institution, Washington, D. C.

Indian moccasins were usually ankle-height, had a rawhide sole and uppers of soft buckskin, but some northern and Mississippi Valley tribes wore a soft-soled moccasin.

They were usually painted and often decorated with fur, porcupine quills, and skin fringes around the ankles and heels. Some tribes used buffalo skin with the hair inside for winter.

Indian Materials You Can Use: Rawhide for soles, soft buckskin, split cowhide. Cowhide is usually sold in half hides from 3 to 5 feet square.

Substitute Materials: Decorate a pair of gym shoes. Use small pieces of soft leather, leatherette, or heavy cloth for heel decoration.

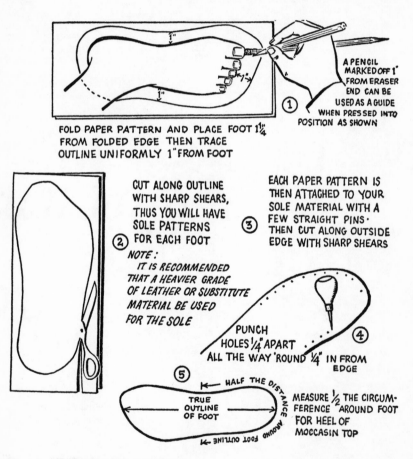

① A PENCIL MARKED OFF 1" FROM ERASER END CAN BE USED AS A GUIDE WHEN PRESSED INTO POSITION AS SHOWN

FOLD PAPER PATTERN AND PLACE FOOT 1¼ FROM FOLDED EDGE THEN TRACE OUTLINE UNIFORMLY 1" FROM FOOT

② CUT ALONG OUTLINE WITH SHARP SHEARS, THUS YOU WILL HAVE SOLE PATTERNS FOR EACH FOOT

NOTE:
IT IS RECOMMENDED THAT A HEAVIER GRADE OF LEATHER OR SUBSTITUTE MATERIAL BE USED FOR THE SOLE

③ EACH PAPER PATTERN IS THEN ATTACHED TO YOUR SOLE MATERIAL WITH A FEW STRAIGHT PINS· THEN CUT ALONG OUTSIDE EDGE WITH SHARP SHEARS

④ PUNCH HOLES ¼" APART ALL THE WAY 'ROUND ¼" IN FROM EDGE

⑤ HALF THE DISTANCE AROUND FOOT OUTLINE
TRUE OUTLINE OF FOOT
MEASURE ½ THE CIRCUMFERENCE AROUND FOOT FOR HEEL OF MOCCASIN TOP

Tools and Equipment You Will Need: Awl, heavy thread, beeswax, darning or upholsterer's needle, cutting shears, pattern paper, pencil or marking crayon.

Indian Decorations: Colored beads, needle and thread, if you plan to bead the top of your moccasin; oil paints, fine brushes, and India ink for painting the tops of your substitute (gym shoes) moccasins.

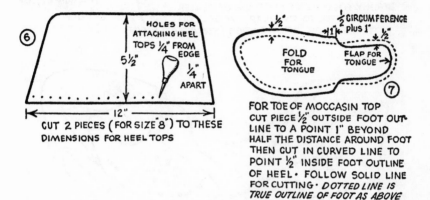

⑥ HOLES FOR ATTACHING HEEL TOPS ¼" FROM EDGE

5½"

¼" APART

|← — — — 12" — — — →|

CUT 2 PIECES (FOR SIZE 8") TO THESE DIMENSIONS FOR HEEL TOPS

½" ½ CIRCUMFERENCE plus 1"

FOLD FOR TONGUE

FLAP FOR TONGUE →

⑦

FOR TOE OF MOCCASIN TOP CUT PIECE ½" OUTSIDE FOOT OUT LINE TO A POINT 1" BEYOND HALF THE DISTANCE AROUND FOOT THEN CUT IN CURVED LINE TO POINT ½" INSIDE FOOT OUTLINE OF HEEL · FOLLOW SOLID LINE FOR CUTTING · *DOTTED LINE IS TRUE OUTLINE OF FOOT AS ABOVE*

Instructions for Making Moccasins: It is best to use rawhide for the soles and soft buckskin for the tops; however, if you desire, you can use buckskin for top and bottom.

Fig. 1 shows how to make a paper pattern.

Fig. 2 explains the cutting of the paper pattern.

Fig. 3 describes the process of pinning the paper pattern on the rawhide sole material and ready for cutting.

Fig. 4 shows how to punch the holes for sewing. They are punched all the way round the sole, ¼ inch apart and ½ inch in from the edge.

Fig. 5 shows how to measure the top heel material.

Fig. 6 is a layout of the top heel material and how to punch holes for sewing.

Fig. 7 gives detailed instructions for cutting the top toe section with flap.

Fig. 8 shows simple process of sewing the sole and top pieces together.

Fig. 9 shows how to insert the thong laces for tying the moccasin.

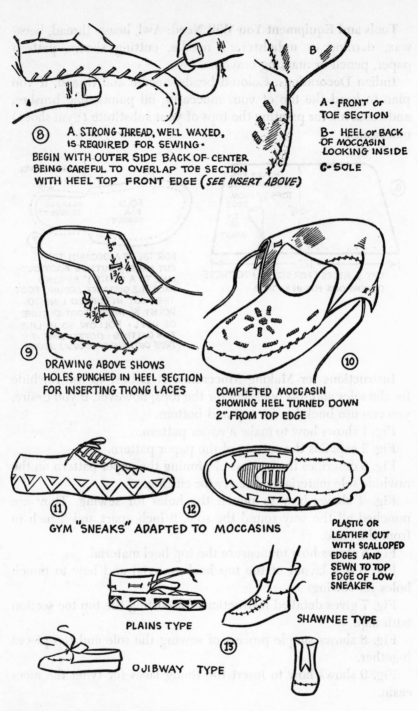

⑧ A. STRONG THREAD, WELL WAXED, IS REQUIRED FOR SEWING. BEGIN WITH OUTER SIDE BACK OF CENTER BEING CAREFUL TO OVERLAP TOE SECTION WITH HEEL TOP FRONT EDGE (*SEE INSERT ABOVE*)

A - FRONT or TOE SECTION

B - HEEL or BACK OF MOCCASIN LOOKING INSIDE

C - SOLE

⑨ DRAWING ABOVE SHOWS HOLES PUNCHED IN HEEL SECTION FOR INSERTING THONG LACES

⑩ COMPLETED MOCCASIN SHOWING HEEL TURNED DOWN 2" FROM TOP EDGE

⑪ ⑫ GYM "SNEAKS" ADAPTED TO MOCCASINS

PLASTIC OR LEATHER CUT WITH SCALLOPED EDGES AND SEWN TO TOP EDGE OF LOW SNEAKER

PLAINS TYPE

SHAWNEE TYPE

⑬ OJIBWAY TYPE

Fig. 10 shows the moccasin ready for wearing with the top heel material turned down.

Fig. 11 is a very satisfactory pair of imitation Indian moccasins made out of a pair of oxford style gym shoes. Quite often they are more comfortable and practical than a hand-made pair of moccasins.

Fig. 12 shows how to add a plastic cloth, or soft leather scalloped decorative edging to the top heel portion of the imitation moccasin.

Fig. 13 shows 3 styles of Indian moccasins.

Indian Decorations: You may wish to add a beaded decoration on your moccasin, as shown in Fig. 10. Use a lazy stitch, as described in Chapter II, Indian Beadwork.

If you make the imitation gym shoe moccasins, they can be decorated by outlining Indian designs with India ink, then filling in the spaces with bright colored oil paints, being careful to stay within the ink lines.

You can also "freckle" or stipple the shoes with dots of bright and vari-colored paints to produce a good imitation of beadwork.

Indian Moccasin Kits: Many styles of moccasins can be quickly and easily made by purchasing a moccasin kit supplied by a number of reliable firms, including:

Soft and hard soled kits—Plume Trading & Sales Co., Box 585, Monroe, N. Y.; Grey Owl, 4518 7th Ave., Brooklyn 20, N. Y.

Plain kits—S. & S. Leather Co., Colchester, Conn.

Brown or white elkskin—Cleveland Crafts Co., 4705 Euclid Ave., Cleveland, O.

Tough steerhide—J. C. Larson Co., 820 South Tripp Ave., Chicago, Ill.

Elkskin, natural, Indian tan, red, white—Kit Kraft, 7373 Melrose Ave., Los Angeles, Calif.

Brown elkskin, combinations of black and white or brown and white tips and colors of short hair calf, and the Carver Kit, easy-to-tool leather, and the easy-to-bead California glove leather—Russo Handcraft Supplies, 245 South Spring St., Los Angeles, Calif.

Sturdy, modern-type—O. H. Dugan & Co., 44 South St., Boston, Mass.

Cowhide—American Handcrafts Co., 302 Throckmorton St., Fort Worth, Texas. Full instructions for making moccasins are usually enclosed with each kit.

"Tuffy-Moc" moccasin kit, Apache Leather Co., 2804 E. Washington, Phoenix, Arizona.

Headcovering: As a general rule, Indian maidens and squaws did not wear any headgear, except for ceremonials, dances, religious, and festive occasions. The beaded headband was not worn by the early Indian woman. Today, you will see a few maidens and squaws wearing a headband for special occasions, and, of course, it is standard practice for many Indian female characters to wear headbands in western and Indian movies!

Pueblo women, particularly in Taos, New Mexico, wear a large shawl over their heads. They are not allowed to go to the village stream for water or work at their bake ovens without a head-covering.

Indian Dress: Since there are so many different styles of Indian dresses, we will confine ourselves to two basic women's garments, influenced in time by the whites. The stereotyped Indian dress reaches from shoulders to the calf or ankle. The early dress was made by simply sewing together two large animal skins, up the sides and across the top, with arm and neck openings, as shown in Fig. 1. In Fig. 2, we see a variation of the long dress as worn by a Winnebago maiden.

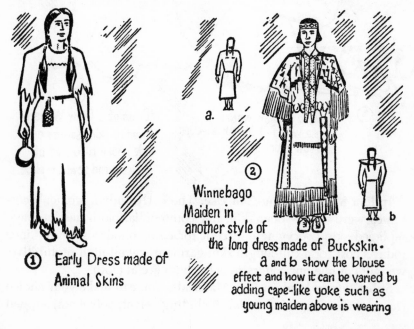

a.

① Early Dress made of Animal Skins

② Winnebago Maiden in another style of the long dress made of Buckskin. a and b show the blouse effect and how it can be varied by adding cape-like yoke such as young maiden above is wearing

b

The second stereotype dress is a blouse-sleeve and full skirt, worn by many eastern and Plains women, as shown in Fig. 3. The early skirts were cut from one or two animal skins. The modern Indian maiden and squaw likes to make her blouse out of many kinds of bright colored materials. They are usually plain square cut or have a large ruffled collar, as shown in Fig. 2, a and b.

The Crow women added a cape-like yoke effect to their early dress of two animal skins, as shown in Fig. 4.

Fig. 7 is a Shawnee dress, and Fig. 8 is a Pueblo costume.

Indian maidens exercised much imagination in decorating their garments, including the use of beads, quills, elk teeth, shells, etc.

③ Navaho woman wearing blouse with full-length sleeves and Full Skirt

④ Dress of a Crow Woman· An entire skin used for each side· Yoke is formed of 2 pieces and sewed in place.

Indian Materials You Can Use: The early Indian women's costumes were mostly deer skin, but commercial cloth has long ago replaced skin everywhere, except for ceremonial costumes. Since today's cost for a full-length skin garment is well-nigh prohibitive, we will confine our suggestions to commercial cloth.

Substitute or Modern-Day Materials: You can make your choice from a wide range of materials including velvet, velveteen, napped suedecloth, wool felt cloth, sateen, cotton, wool, denim, ticking, indianhead, linen, unbleached muslin, monks cloth, and crash. Be sure to dye or buy bright colored materials.

In the western trading posts one can buy the most beautiful and colorful modern-styled Indian dress made of two fabulous fabrics called Egyptian cotton and silk georgette. Why it cannot be readily found in other parts of the country is a mystery to the author.

Tools and Equipment You Will Need: Dry cleaners paper garment bag or newspapers for pattern. Scissors, needle, thread, measuring tape, and straight pins.

Indian Decorations: Nowadays some Pueblo women trim the bottom of their sleeved garments with lace. The Hopis decorate the edgings of the dresses with patterns woven in the fabric or embroidered with red, blue or green wool. Of course, much silver, shell, and turquoise jewelry is worn with most of the Indian women's costumes.

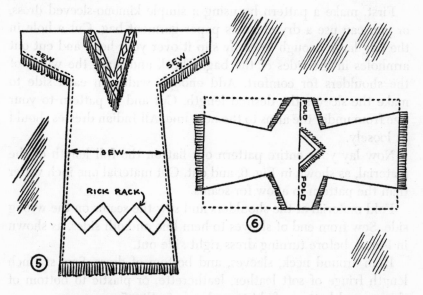

Costume of Plains woman showing simple one piece construction and where to apply fringe for decoration

The southern Plains blouses and sleeves were limited to narrow painted or beaded edgings.

The central Plains blouse and cape-sleeves were almost completely covered with solid beading.

Colored bands were sewn on the northern Plains sleeves and around the bottom of the blouse.

Beads, quills, rows of pendant thongs, elks teeth, shells, and tin jingles were added ornaments.

Substitute Decorations: Crayons, colored pencils, oil paints, quick-drying lacquers, poster paints, ribbons, colored yarn, jingle bells, etc.

Instructions for Making Indian Dress: Refer to Fig. 2. First, decide on the kind of material you wish to use. Perhaps you will want to dye your own material, such as unbleached muslin, to simulate leather. If so, refer to Chapter 4, Indian Arts and Decorations, How to make Indian Dyes and Paints.

Your material should be twice the length from your shoulders to your calf or ankle. You will need approximately 3½ yards of 36-inch material.

First, make a pattern by using a simple kimono-sleeved dress, or you can use a dry cleaners paper garment bag. Cut a hole in the bag large enough to easily slip it over your head and cut out armholes in the sides of the bag. Check and mark the width of the shoulders for comfort. Add enough width on each side to make the sleeves the desired length. Cut and fit pattern to your size from under the arms to the hem line. All Indian dresses should fit loosely.

Now lay your entire pattern out flat on the full length of the material, as shown in Fig. 6, and cut. Cut material one inch wider than the pattern to allow for seams.

Fold material at the shoulders and sew the seams on the wrong side. Sew from end of sleeves to hem line on both sides, as shown in Fig. 5, before turning dress right side out.

Hem around neck, sleeves, and bottom of dress. Sew six inch length fringe of soft leather, leatherette, or plastic to bottom of sleeves and bottom of skirt, as shown in Fig. 5.

Sew decorated bands to form a triangle on front of dress at the neck, as shown in Fig. 5. If fringe is desired on the decorative bands, sew it on the bands before sewing them on the dress.

Decorating Your Dress: Refer to Chapter 4, INDIAN ARTS AND DECORATIONS, How to Use Indian Symbols, Designs, and Motifs. Pick out the designs that strike your fancy, and arrange them on paper before outlining them on the triangular-shaped strips of material. You may wish to bead the bands. If so, refer to Chapter 2, Indian Ornaments and Accessories, How to Make Indian Beadwork. You may use rick-rack (twisted tape bought by the yard) as

Shawnee Maiden

Pueblo Girl

a modern decoration for your skirt. Many interesting Indian designs can be made with rick-rack, as it comes in many colors. The triangle-shaped bands at the neck can be beaded or painted with quick-drying lacquers.

REFERENCES: *Indian Leaflet Series,* No's. 108 and 109; Department of Indian Art, Denver Art Museum, Denver, Colorado.

WAR BONNET

War bonnets were worn by men only. They appeared first in North America among the tribes on the Plains between the Rockies and the Mississippi Valley, and by some tribes bordering this area; although they have been adopted by Woodland and Southwestern Tribes.

There are two well-known types of war bonnets. The most colorful, and sometimes called the most beautiful headgear in the world, has the feathers leaning toward the rear, as shown in Fig. 1, worn by the central and southern Plains Indians. Fig. 2, is a "straight-up" bonnet, made without a skullcap, worn by the Blackfoot tribe.

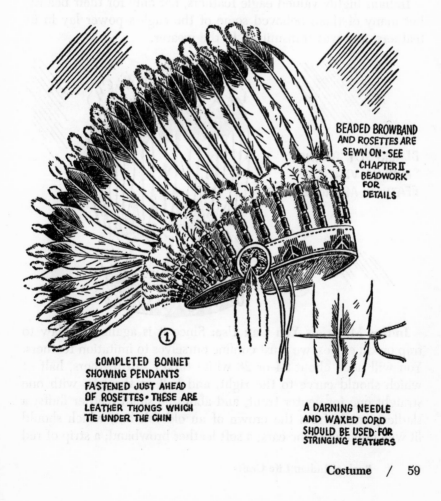

BEADED BROWBAND AND ROSETTES ARE SEWN ON · SEE CHAPTER II "BEADWORK" FOR DETAILS

①

COMPLETED BONNET SHOWING PENDANTS FASTENED JUST AHEAD OF ROSETTES · THESE ARE LEATHER THONGS WHICH TIE UNDER THE CHIN

A DARNING NEEDLE AND WAXED CORD SHOULD BE USED· FOR STRINGING FEATHERS

The war bonnet was worn by men only in recognition of out-standing deeds and for courage in time of war. It was worn during battle or raids and for full-dress ceremonial occasions.

A less-known bonnet, worn by the Apache, has the feathers drooping out evenly all the way around the head, as shown in Fig. 3.

In Fig. 4, we see how Indians, who won more honor feathers than they could put in their head-sized war bonnet, were permitted to make and wear a single or double row of feathers hanging down the back.

Some Indian leaders combined buffalo horns with feathers for a buffalo headdress, as shown in Fig. 5. Fig. A, shows how horns are attached and connected with each other.

Indians highly valued eagle feathers, not only for their beauty, but many of them believed some of the eagle's power lay in its feathers, and was transmitted to the wearer.

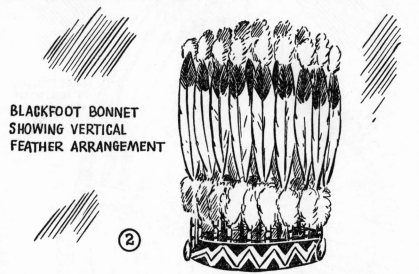

BLACKFOOT BONNET
SHOWING VERTICAL
FEATHER ARRANGEMENT

②

Indian Materials You Can Use: Since it is against the law to trap or kill eagles, we must confine ourselves to imitation feathers. You will need about 24 or 28 white turkey tail feathers, half of which should curve to the right, and half to the left, with one straight one for center front, and about 30 small feather fluffs; a skullcap made from the crown of an old felt hat, which should fit well down over the ears; a soft leather browband; a strip of red felt two yards long and two and a half inches wide; twenty-eight feet of yellow wool yarn and fourteen feet of turquoise blue yarn; enough leather thong for lacing the feathers around the skullcap.

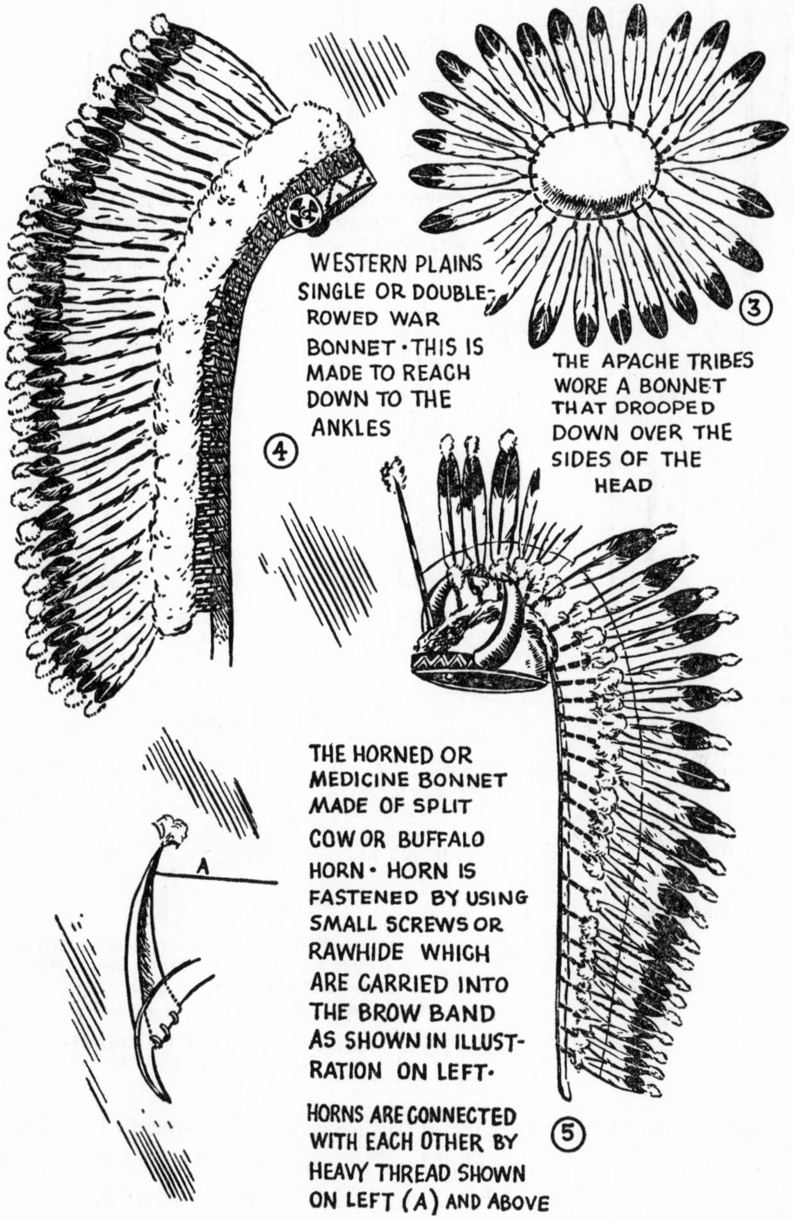

WESTERN PLAINS SINGLE OR DOUBLE-ROWED WAR BONNET · THIS IS MADE TO REACH DOWN TO THE ANKLES ④

THE APACHE TRIBES WORE A BONNET THAT DROOPED DOWN OVER THE SIDES OF THE HEAD ③

THE HORNED OR MEDICINE BONNET MADE OF SPLIT COW OR BUFFALO HORN · HORN IS FASTENED BY USING SMALL SCREWS OR RAWHIDE WHICH ARE CARRIED INTO THE BROW BAND AS SHOWN IN ILLUSTRATION ON LEFT·

HORNS ARE CONNECTED WITH EACH OTHER BY HEAVY THREAD SHOWN ON LEFT (A) AND ABOVE ⑤

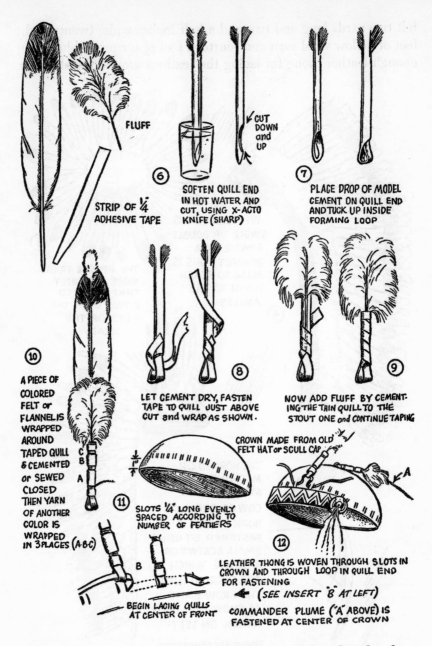

FLUFF

STRIP OF ¼
ADHESIVE TAPE

6 SOFTEN QUILL END
IN HOT WATER AND
CUT, USING X-ACTO
KNIFE (SHARP)

CUT
DOWN
and
UP

7 PLACE DROP OF MODEL
CEMENT ON QUILL END
AND TUCK UP INSIDE
FORMING LOOP

10 A PIECE OF
COLORED
FELT or
FLANNEL IS
WRAPPED
AROUND
TAPED QUILL
& CEMENTED
or SEWED
CLOSED
THEN YARN
OF ANOTHER
COLOR IS
WRAPPED
IN 3 PLACES (A·B·C)

8 LET CEMENT DRY, FASTEN
TAPE TO QUILL JUST ABOVE
CUT and WRAP AS SHOWN.

9 NOW ADD FLUFF BY CEMENT-
ING THE THIN QUILL TO THE
STOUT ONE and CONTINUE TAPING

CROWN MADE FROM OLD
FELT HAT or SCULL CAP

11 SLOTS ¼" LONG EVENLY
SPACED ACCORDING TO
NUMBER OF FEATHERS

12 LEATHER THONG IS WOVEN THROUGH SLOTS IN
CROWN AND THROUGH LOOP IN QUILL END
FOR FASTENING
◀ (SEE INSERT "B" AT LEFT)
COMMANDER PLUME ("A" ABOVE) IS
FASTENED AT CENTER OF CROWN

B

BEGIN LACING QUILLS
AT CENTER OF FRONT

Substitute Materials: All the Indian materials listed in the above
paragraph are readily available. The only substitute material you
may wish to use would be an imitation bead browband.

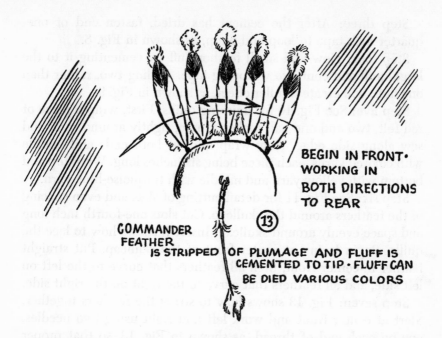

BEGIN IN FRONT·
WORKING IN
BOTH DIRECTIONS
TO REAR

COMMANDER
FEATHER
IS STRIPPED OF PLUMAGE AND FLUFF IS
CEMENTED TO TIP · FLUFF CAN
BE DIED VARIOUS COLORS

⑬

Tools and Equipment You Will Need: Measuring tape or foot ruler, marking pencil, X-acto knife, scissors, roll of one quarter inch adhesive tape or scotch tape, darning needles, heavy waxed thread or cord, model cement.

Indian Decorations: Strip of beaded browband, ten inches long and one inch wide, leather thong, rabbit tails, two pieces of soft leather for two and a quarter inch diameter rosettes, and colored beads for decorating rosettes.

Substitute Decorations: Strip of commercial imitation beadwork for browband, ten inches long and one inch wide. In place of beaded rosettes, you can use a pom-pom made with a piece of cardboard, heavy foil, cardboard or foil milk tops, or the tops of small frozen fruit cans. You can decorate pom-pom with crayons, colored pencils, oil paints, quick-drying lacquers, water or poster paints, ribbons, colored yarn.

Instructions for Making War Bonnet: Refer to Figs. 6-13.

Step one: Soften quill end of feather in hot water and cut it as shown in Fig. 6.

Step two: Place a drop of model cement on end of quill and tuck up inside quill, forming a loop, Fig. 7.

Step three: After the cement has dried, fasten end of one-quarter inch tape to loop and wrap, as shown in Fig. 8.

Step four: Now add small feather fluff by cementing it to the large quill and continue wrapping tape. Adding two, rather than one fluff, will create a fuller effect, as shown in Fig. 9.

Step five: See Fig. 10 for finishing quills. First, wrap a piece of red felt, two and one-half inches square, tightly around quill and sew along side edge. Now wrap quill at both ends and middle with colored yarns, each piece being six inches long. Wrap top and bottom with yellow yarn and middle with turquoise-blue yarn.

Step six: See Fig. 11 for detail cutting of slots and even spacing of the feathers around the skullcap. Cut slots one-fourth inch long and space evenly around skullcap. Insert B shows how to lace the quills. Begin lacing at center front of the skullcap. Put straight feather in center front, then all feathers that curve to the left on left side, and all feathers that curve to the right on the right side.

Step seven: Fig. 13 shows how to string the feathers together. Start at center front and work left and right using two needles, one on each end of thread, as shown in Fig. 13, so that proper adjustment can be made at the back. Adjust and space all feathers evenly before knotting the ends of the thread. Use heavy waxed thread or cord.

Step eight: Cement fluffs to tip of feathers with model cement.

Step nine: Sew strip of beaded browband to front of headdress, as shown in Fig. 12. Refer to Chapter 2 for beadwork details.

Step ten: Sew rosettes to sides of skullcap, add rabbit tails and thongs for decorations, as shown in Fig. 1. Refer to Chapter 2, Indian Ornaments and Accessories, for detailed construction of beaded rosettes. If you wish to substitute poms-poms for the rosettes, refer to Chapter 1, the section Headbands of this chapter, for construction details.

Step eleven: See Fig. 13 for adding commander feather to crown of headdress. Strip all plumage off large feather. Now, cement various colored fluffs to tip of stripped quill and sew quill to top or crown of headdress. You may take white fluffs and dye them the desired different colors. The completed war bonnet is shown in Fig. 1.

2. ORNAMENTS AND ACCESSORIES

ORNAMENTS

T HE early Indian, without the aid of modern machinery, had to study his raw materials very carefully in order to create simple but beautiful and eye-catching ornaments. In the beginning the Indians used a simple collection of natural objects or applied color on their bodies. This was followed by ornaments attached to their clothing and personal belongings. Ornaments were added to the hair, pins, plugs, and pendants to the ears, and encircling bands to the waists, arms and legs. Decorated Indian objects included objects of stone, wood, bone, horn and shell: totem poles, dwellings, masks, pipes, implements, utensils, pottery, jewelry, ceremonial equipment, baskets, etc.

Ornaments were made from mineral, vegetable or animal substances. Some early mineral substances used for ornaments included copper, quartz, slate, soapstone, and turquoise. Later they included silver, porcelain, and glass. Vegetable substances included seeds, nuts, stems, and roots. Animal materials included shell, bone, horn, teeth, and claws.

Northwest Coast Indian Ornaments: The Northwest Indian men wore ear and nose pendants of wood, feathers, shell and metal. They oiled their hair and sprinkled it with red ochre, mica and shiny sand. White bird down was scattered over the hair.

Pueblo Indian Ornaments: Both sexes wore much jewelry, silver necklaces, belts, bracelets, rings, buttons, etc., made chiefly by the Navahos and Zunis, and necklaces and earrings of shell and turquoise.

The Plains Indian Ornaments: The men wore many kinds of decorations on the head, usually of feathers, fur, hair, quills, or beads. The women wore belts around the waist over the dress. They were wider than those worn by the men and were decorated with beads, brass nails, and discs. Pouches and bags hung from the belt.

REFERENCES: *Indian Leaflet Series,* No. 1, 4, & 24, Denver Art Museum, Denver, Colo.

Bull. 30, p. 149, Bureau of American Ethnology, Smithsonian Institution, Washington, D. C.

The suggestions for making Indian belts, shown in Fig. 1, 2 and 3, will give you an idea of the many kinds of belts you can make. The Indian was a master craftsman because he made use of the many things that he found in nature and all about him. Making an Indian belt offers you an excellent opportunity to use your original ideas. Many kinds of material are available for making handsome belts, and many fine belt kits are on the market. Leather craft, for instance, is an absorbing and satisfying hobby. Making a leather belt is an excellent project for the beginner. Just make sure that your final project is "Indian looking."

Materials You Can Use: Leather, cigar box, balsa or hard woods (even a yard stick), plastic, cork, copper, brass and aluminum can be used for making "blocks" which can be linked together with leather thong, gimp, or shoe lacing. You can use the tops of small frozen fruit cans for disks.

Tools and Equipment You Will Need: Small coping saw for cutting wood blocks, sharp knife for cutting leather blocks, shears for cutting metal blocks; hammer and large nail for punching or dotting designs on the metal blocks, or you may prefer to use a wood-burning set; oil paints or lacquers for painting the blocks.

Indian Decorations: Fig. 2 shows you how to use the tops of small frozen fruit cans to make disks. Circular pieces can be cut with small metal shears to form a scalloped edge. The eyes of the

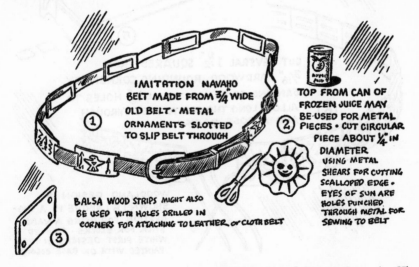

1. IMITATION NAVAHO BELT MADE FROM ¾" WIDE OLD BELT · METAL ORNAMENTS SLOTTED TO SLIP BELT THROUGH

2. TOP FROM CAN OF FROZEN JUICE MAY BE USED FOR METAL PIECES · CUT CIRCULAR PIECE ABOUT ¼" IN DIAMETER USING METAL SHEARS FOR CUTTING SCALLOPED EDGE · EYES OF SUN ARE HOLES PUNCHED THROUGH METAL FOR SEWING TO BELT

3. BALSA WOOD STRIPS MIGHT ALSO BE USED WITH HOLES DRILLED IN CORNERS FOR ATTACHING TO LEATHER, or CLOTH BELT

sun can be punched through for sewing the disk on to the belt.

You can stamp or dot Indian designs on the metal blocks with a hammer and large nail, as shown in Fig. 4, or you may prefer to use a wood-burning set for putting your designs on the wood blocks, as indicated in Fig. 6.

You might like to paint your Indian designs on the wood blocks with bright colored oil paints or lacquers.

Fig. 5 shows how to cut belt blocks out of a yard stick.

If you have plenty of patience and time, you can make an Indian beaded belt. Make your strip of beadwork on a loom, and sew it to the belt material, as shown in Fig. 22 on page 75.

Many good belt kits are available on the market, but don't hesitate to use your imagination in creating your very own ideas, making sure to use good Indian designs.

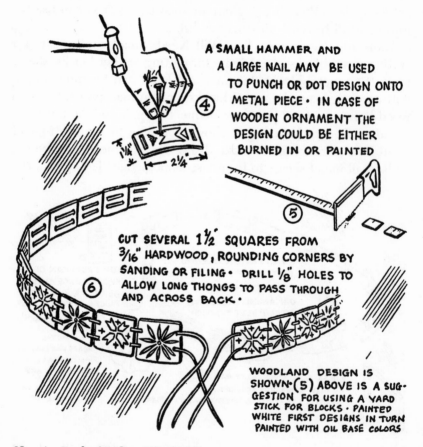

A SMALL HAMMER AND A LARGE NAIL MAY BE USED TO PUNCH OR DOT DESIGN ONTO METAL PIECE · IN CASE OF WOODEN ORNAMENT THE DESIGN COULD BE EITHER BURNED IN OR PAINTED

④

⑤

CUT SEVERAL 1½" SQUARES FROM 3/16" HARDWOOD, ROUNDING CORNERS BY SANDING OR FILING · DRILL ⅛" HOLES TO ALLOW LONG THONGS TO PASS THROUGH AND ACROSS BACK ·

⑥

WOODLAND DESIGN IS SHOWN·(5) ABOVE IS A SUGGESTION FOR USING A YARD STICK FOR BLOCKS · PAINTED WHITE FIRST DESIGNS IN TURN PAINTED WITH OIL BASE COLORS

Belt-craft Supply Houses:

The Handcrafters, Waupun, Wisconsin.

Zuni Indian belt kit, Tandy Leather Co., 300 Throckmorton St., Fort Worth, Texas.

Copper foil—American Handcrafts Co., 12 E. 41st St., New York, N. Y.

Copper cutouts—Magnus Craft Materials, 108 Franklin St., New York 13, N. Y.

Leather belt blocks and leather block kits—Cleveland Crafts Co., Cleveland, 3, Ohio.

Apache Leather Co., 2804 E. Washington, Phoenix, Arizona.

Link Belt kits, complete with 6 leather links, shaped and punched; 1 round leather buckle; 2⅛" Indian tanned lacing thongs, 54" long; patterns & instructions.

Plastic belt kits—S. & S. Leather Co., Inc., Colchester, Conn.

Complete supply of copper and brass materials for the craftsman—Groundmaster Co., Boulder, Colo.

BIBLIOGRAPHY: *General Leathercraft*, Raymond Cherry, McKnight & McKnight Publishing Company, Bloomington, Ill.

Indians were well-known for their mastery of stringing ornaments, pendants, and beads around the neck and wrists, and attaching them to their garments.

They were made from mineral, vegetable, or animal substances before the introduction of glass and porcelain beads by the white man.

Nuts and berries were strung, and it has been reported that the Mandan and other Missouri tribes pounded and melted glass and molded it into beads.

Before the introduction of European seed beads, the Plains and Woodland Indians used dyed porcupine quills.

The Pueblo Indians strung sections of woody stems of plants, seashells and varieties of bright colored stones.

In addition, the skin was tattooed, colors were applied, feathers and other articles were added to the hair. Pins, plugs and pendants were added to the ears and encircling bands to the waist, ankles, arms, and legs.

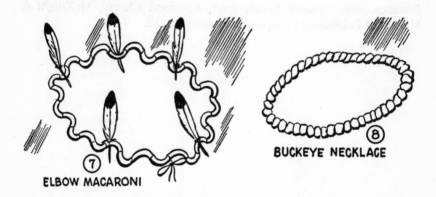

ELBOW MACARONI

BUCKEYE NECKLACE

Materials for Making Necklace: Native materials: Nuts, clay, teeth, claws, seeds, shells, buckeyes (horse chestnuts), dried corn, small bones, bamboo stems, small feathers, glass and wood beads, and bright bits of cloth.

Yellow or Ring Top Cowrie shells make a a fine necklace. Pink conch shells, also known as moon shells, make a good-looking necklace. Drill holes in shells with a hard drill and small bit.

Substitute Materials: Dried raisins, elbow macaroni, colored

ROPE OF SEED BEADS ⑨

⑩ NECKBAND or CHOKER

⑪ BAMBOO PIPE STEMS and WOODEN BEADS

⑫ CLAW & BEAD NECKLACE
(USING BALSA WOOD FOR CLAWS)

⑬ SEA SHELLS (COWRIE)

⑭ OLD SEWING SPOOLS

buttons, thick mixture of modeling clay, and balsa wood for imitation claws and teeth; small thread spools.

Tools and Equipment You Will Need: Knife scissors, heavy thread or jewelry wire, needle, crayons, water colors or oil paints. Colored food dyes.

Instructions for Making Necklace: Fig. 7 is an imitation bone necklace made with elbow macaroni and small bird feathers. Paint the macaroni with egg-shell white to resemble bone, or use bright colored oil paints or poster paints.

Fig. 8 is an attractive buckeye (horse chestnut) necklace.

Fig. 9 is a six or more looped strand of glass or wooden beads.

Fig. 10 is a beaded neckband. See Chapter II on beadwork, for details.

Fig. 11 is an imitation bone necklace made out of bamboo pipe stems that can be obtained in any cigar store or Indian trading post. Paint the stems an egg-shell white for bone effect.

Fig. 12 is an imitation claw or tooth necklace. Carve these out of balsa wood, or, if you are a good whittler, use soft wood. Paint them an egg-shell white to look like teeth; shade with black paint, if you wish, to look like claws.

Fig. 13 is a necklace made with cowrie sea shells. Drill a small hole in each shell, or you can buy drilled shells from the Plume Trading & Sales Co., P.O. Box 585, Monroe, New York.

Fig. 14 is a necklace made of thread spools. Chip the ends of the spools with a sharp knife and decorate them with bright colored paints.

You can string a nice looking Pueblo necklace with Indian corn, or you can string Florida Black-eyed Susan beans.

BEADWORK

Beadwork began after the discovery of America, and was preceded by porcupine quill embroidery. Pearls and shells were also used as decorative materials before glass beads were introduced. Large glass beads were brought to this country by early Italian explorers.

Most Indian beadwork was done in the central and southern Plains and the Northern and Woodland sections.

Glass beads come from Europe, including Italy, Czecho-Slovakia, France, Germany, and Japan.

Early beads made from clams, conch, and periwinkle were called "wampum," which was used by the colonists as a medium of exchange in place of money. Glass beads were accepted as trade for furs.

In late 1600, a small bead about 3/32" in diameter, called the "pony" bead, was introduced for beadwork. It was uneven in shape and size and white and blue in color.

Beads were also used for legal money in Dutch and English settlements.

Clark Wissler, in his American Museum of Natural History Science Guide No. 63, tells us that the oldest piece of North American beadwork is a skin robe in the Ashmolean Museum, Oxford, England, attributed to Powhatan, a famous Indian who lived in Virginia about 1607. Native shell beads, attached with sinew thread, were used in this embroidery. (In passing, this author can't help but express a deep feeling of chagrin that such a valuable piece of early Americana must repose in a foreign museum!)

There are three ways of making sewn beadwork. Beads may be sewn singly; several at a time (known as the lazy stitch), shown in Fig. 80, page 54; or they may be appliqued.

Rosettes for the war bonnet are made by applying beads to a circular piece of heavy cloth or soft leather, beginning in the center with one bead. Graduating rows of beads are then sewn around this central bead until the desired size rosette is completed. At the end of each circle, the row will be more even if you run your thread through the entire row of beads again. Many designs may be made by using variously colored beads according to a prearranged plan.

The applique method of applying beads is accomplished by stringing beads on a thread and then, using a second needle and thread, tacking down the string of beads at close intervals. This method of beading was used by the Woodland Indians for floral design beadwork.

A study of Plains and Woodland beadwork will reveal that many neighboring tribes used different methods of weaving; and other tribes, separated by thousands of miles, were using the same method of beading.

In general, Indian beadwork designs were geometrical and floral. Two types of patterns were introduced from Europe, the double-curve and floral, and these spread widely from coast to coast through influence of the fur trade, transcontinental highways and railroads, and government removal of tribes. Oriental rug designs affected Sioux beadwork in the 1860's and have been used ever since.

THE OJIBWA BEAD LOOM

The Ojibwa Bead Loom, Fig. 15, can be purchased as a kit from the Plume Trading & Sales Co., Monroe, N. Y. It is made up of two dowel rods and two notched end pieces, plus four screw-eyes. We recommend it because it will hold enough beadwork to produce a full legging strip or a strip for the war shirt, as well as for shorter pieces.

How to Use the Ojibwa Loom: For a long bead strip, and for a belt, insert the ends of the dowel rods in the holes in the end pieces, and tighten the screw eyes. See Fig. 15.

String the loom with No. 8 thread (linen, if you can get it, or well-waxed cotton). Start this by fastening the end of the thread to the screw nearest you at the left end when the loom is standing before you. Use a slip knot, as this will have to be untied later.

If, for example, your beadwork is to be 17 beads wide, then string 18 strings; and we have found through long experience, that making the outer strands double helps a lot, especially where the beadwork is later to be sewn onto a backing.

Bring the thread up as in Fig. 16 and place it in the third or fourth notch, bring it across the loom to the corresponding notch at the other end, down under the loom, and finally up and through the next notch. Continue this around and around until the de-

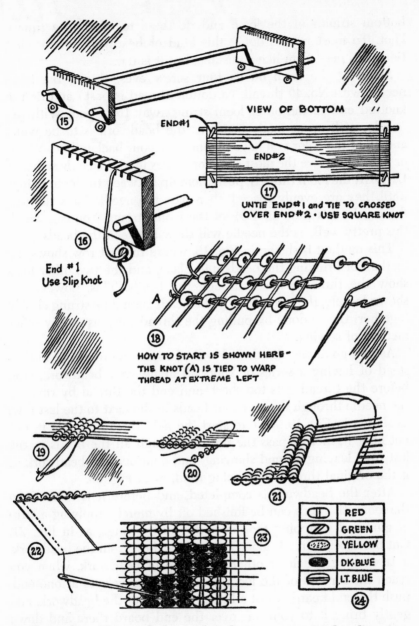

VIEW OF BOTTOM

END#1

END#2

⑮

⑰

UNTIE END#1 and TIE TO CROSSED OVER END#2 · USE SQUARE KNOT

⑯

End #1
Use Slip Knot

A

⑱

HOW TO START IS SHOWN HERE—
THE KNOT (A) IS TIED TO WARP
THREAD AT EXTREME LEFT

⑲

⑳

㉑

㉒

㉓

RED	
GREEN	
YELLOW	
DK·BLUE	
LT. BLUE	

㉔

sired number of strands have thus been strung. Make the turns as tight as possible, without breaking the thread.

When this is completed, untie the beginning, end #1, from the screw, bring the final end, end #2, as in Fig. 17, across the bottom strands of the loom and tie these together in a square knot. To most people doing this kind of beadwork for the first time, this may seem like a mistake, but it is not.

Standing the loom on its four screw eyes, thread the bead needle with No. 40 thread, (a double thread is best) and tie the knotted end to the outer loom string away from you. With the needle, pick up as many beads as the beadwork is to be wide, and all of the color you have planned for your background. White or light blue were the most common colors used. Place these beads UNDER the loom threads, push them up between the loom strings until they are evenly spaced, then pass the needle back through the beads, this time on TOP of the loom strings. You can watch this pretty well, as the needle will show between the beads.

This method is shown in Fig. 18, where the last row shows the method of bringing the beads into place, and the two other lines show the thread passed through the beads. This, however, is shown loosely, though naturally the beads should be strung closely together; this is done by pulling the thread tight as in any other method of sewing.

As you go along, the thread will of course be used up; but instead of having a series of knots all along your beadwork, stop before the thread gets too short, and end the thread by running the needle through three or four beads in the next to the last row, as shown in Fig. 19. Also, to start the next thread, double it, but not knot it, merely pass the needle through all the beads in the last row, leaving an end showing, and continue the beadwork as if the original thread were being used, as in Fig. 20.

After the beadwork is completed, and before it is taken from the loom, the ends can be finished off by merely applying a strip of gummed wrapping tape over the loom strings, as in Fig. 21. Cut the excess threads along the tape farthest from the beadwork.

In making a belt or other long strip of beadwork, when you reach the far end of the loom, loosen the screw eyes at one end, push the end board in just a little, take hold of the beadwork, and gently bring it to your left over the end board there and down under the loom. When you thus have a new set of loom threads on top of the loom again, place your thumb on the end of the dowel rod at the loose end and with the two first fingers gently pull the end board towards the thumb. When the loom strings are tight, apply the screw eye again into the end board. Repeat this method on the other dowel rod. You will now see that the crossed thread is getting into line, and will eventually straighten itself out.

When sewing the finished beadwork to a leather belt or to the part of your costume where it is to be worn, start at one end, sew about six inches down along one side, then do the same along the other side, as this helps to make the beadwork lay smoothly. Finally, tuck the ends with the gummed tape under the bead-work, thus hiding it, and sew across this between the last two rows of beads as shown in Fig. 22.

Fig. 23 shows how to draw a design on graph paper, and also how to arrive at a square in beads. As the beads are oval and not round, it takes a group of three beads wide by four high to make a square. Therefore, also, in using graph paper it is suggested that you use two squares wide by one deep for each bead.

Fig. 24 shows how you can indicate colors if crayons or water-colors are not at hand.

After the first row of beads is in place, the going is not so hard, and then the interesting part begins, because as you now pick up beads of a number of different colors to produce the design, each new row makes the design grow, and the more you do the more you will enjoy it.

For shorter pieces of beadwork you can save thread by merely bringing one of the end pieces farther in on the two dowel rods.

The booklet, American Indian Beadwork Designs, compiled by Gray-Wolf, Plume Trading & Sales Co., Inc., P. O. Box 585, Monroe, N. Y., is an excellent guide for the beginner and the advanced beadworker.

REFERENCES: *Indian Leaflet Series*, No. 2, 31, 73-74, 117 and 118-119, Department of Indian Art, Denver Art Museum, Denver, Colorado.
American Indian Beadwork Designs, Gray-Wolf, Plume Trading & Sales Co., Inc., Monroe, New York.
Beadwork, Bull. 30, page 137-139, Bureau of American Ethnology, Washington, D. C.
Science Guide No. 63, Clark Wissler, American Museum of Natural History, New York, N. Y.
Looms: Ojibwa Bead Loom, Plume Trading & Sales Co., Box 585, Monroe, N. Y.; Grey Owl Indian Craft Co., 4518 7th Ave., Brooklyn 20, N. Y.; Walco Bead Co., 37 W. 37th St., New York 18, N. Y.

Beadcraft sets: X-ACTO, Inc., 48–41 Van Dam St., Long Island City 1, New York. *Also hobby shops, stores, and trading posts.*

BIBLIOGRAPHY: *The Golden Book of Indian Crafts and Lore,* W. Ben Hunt, Simon & Schuster, New York, N. Y.

The Book of Indian Crafts and Indian Lore, J. H. Solomon, Harper & Brothers, New York, N. Y.

Indian bags and pouches were made of soft skin. The Plains Indians used geometrical designs and the Woodland Indians used floral designs on their bags and pouches. Many Indians will not tell you what the designs mean because they want to keep it a secret. Your interpretation of the design may be entirely different from that of the Indian, so make up your own design and keep it a secret just as the Indians do.

Indian Materials You Can Use: A piece of soft leather or chamois cloth, size 10″ x 14″, and a strip of leather fringe, 1″ wide and 18″ long.

Substitute Materials: Canvas, felt, plastic, flannel, imitation leather or double-napped suede.

Tools and Equipment You Will Need: Needle, foot rule, marking pencil, linen thread No. 20, scissors, leather thong 40″ long for draw-cord.

Indian Decorations: Beadwork, fringe edging, vegetable, berry or root dyes.

Substitute Decorations: Crayons, colored pencils, oil paints, quick-drying lacquers, colored yarn or bits of colored cloth for applique (sewn) work.

Instructions for Making Your Pouch: First, cut the piece of leather or chamois in half, so you will have 2 pieces 5″ x 7″. Lay one piece on top of the other, and cut round corners, as shown in Fig. 25. Now sew the two pieces together on the wrong side with a ¼″ seam, as shown in Fig. 26. If fringe is used, you may insert it between the two pieces of pouch on the right side before sewing the seam.

Now cut the slits at the top of your pouch to insert the drawstring or leather thongs. The drawstring or leather thongs are used to close the pouch and also make a handle with which to carry it. Cut 4 slits, ½″ long in each side of pouch. Cut them ⅜″ from the top, as shown in Fig. 2. Cut your 40″ piece of thong or drawstring in two pieces 20″ each. Run them in and out through the slits in opposite directions so one will meet at one end of pouch, and the other one at the other end, as shown in Fig. 2. Tie the two ends of each thong or drawstring together with a knot.

Decorating Your Pouch: Refer to Chapter 4, How to Use Indian Symbols, Designs, and Motifs. Choose your favorite or regional tribal designs and carefully decorate your pouch.

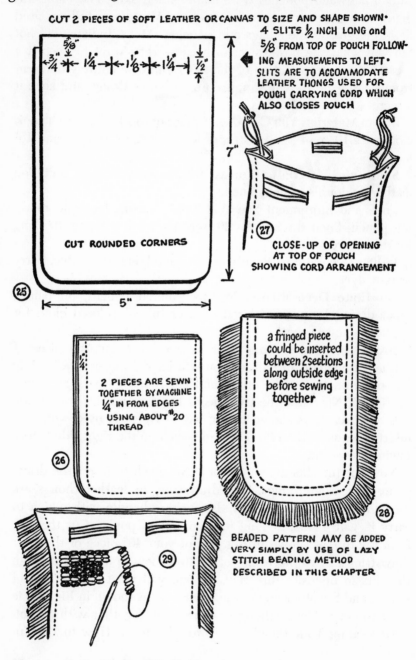

CUT 2 PIECES OF SOFT LEATHER OR CANVAS TO SIZE AND SHAPE SHOWN·
4 SLITS ½ INCH LONG and
⅝ FROM TOP OF POUCH FOLLOWING MEASUREMENTS TO LEFT·
SLITS ARE TO ACCOMMODATE LEATHER THONGS USED FOR POUCH CARRYING CORD WHICH ALSO CLOSES POUCH

⅝"
¾" ¼" 1⅛" 1¼" ½"

7"

CUT ROUNDED CORNERS

② CLOSE-UP OF OPENING
AT TOP OF POUCH
SHOWING CORD ARRANGEMENT

㉕

5"

¼"

2 PIECES ARE SEWN TOGETHER BY MACHINE ¼" IN FROM EDGES USING ABOUT #20 THREAD

㉖

a fringed piece could be inserted between 2 sections along outside edge before sewing together

㉘

㉙

BEADED PATTERN MAY BE ADDED VERY SIMPLY BY USE OF LAZY STITCH BEADING METHOD DESCRIBED IN THIS CHAPTER

Figures 28 and 29 show you how to add fringe and beadwork decorations.

If you decide to paint your pouch, be sure to allow one color to dry before applying another. Use bright colors.

If you plan to decorate your designs with crayon, be sure to iron the backside of the pouch material to melt the wax, which will eliminate smearing.

You might outline your design in pencil and sew it with colored yarn.

You might wish to use cut-out bits of Indian-designed colored cloth or felt and applique (sew) them directly on the pouch.

INDIAN PARFLECHE
(*pronounced "parflesh"*)

The Plains Indians used a Parfleche to carry and store dried meats, berries, tallow, etc. The Indian made a mixture of dried buffalo meat and cherries called "pemmican," which was stored in the parfleche. They also used it to carry their Indian costume and ceremonial equipment.

Indian Materials You Can Use: Undressed or raw hide.

Substitute Materials: Light canvas or heavy parchment paper.

Tools and Equipment: Scissors or sharp knife, measuring tape, marking crayon, 2 strips of leather thong about 3 inches long and 4 straps 12 inches long.

Indian Decorations: Red, yellow, black, and blue oil paints, lacquer, or crayons.

Instructions for Making Parfleche: Make a paper pattern according to the measurements outlined in Fig. 30. Fold your pattern as outlined by the dotted lines. Punch holes as indicated by the circles.

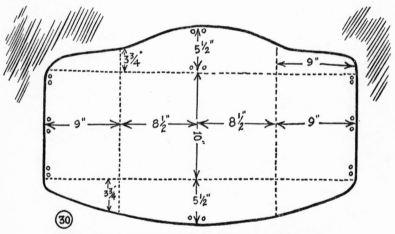

CUT A PIECE OF RAWHIDE OR CANVAS MEASURING
21" X 35" TO THE PATTERN SHOWN ABOVE
(see Text for Directions)
RAWHIDE DOES NOT REQUIRE AN OVERALL COLOR
BUT WHEN CANVAS IS USED IT SHOULD BE PAINTED
A LIGHT CREAM OR BUFF · AFTER PAINT IS THOROUGHLY
DRY, FLAT SURFACE FORMING BACK SHOULD BE DECORATED ·
LOCATE AND PUNCH HOLES AS SHOWN } HOLES

When you are satisfied that your paper pattern fits together neatly, as shown in Fig. 33, you are ready to lay the pattern out flat on the rawhide, canvas, or heavy parchment paper; trace and cut the material, and punch the holes for lacing.

If you prefer to make a larger parfleche, cut your pattern according to the desired length and width, making sure that your overlapping folds fit neatly together before you trace the pattern on the material.

Now tie the parfleche together as illustrated in Fig. 31, beginning with a loop through the holes (B) and following through as indicated by the dotted lines and on through the holes (C) and tie together as shown in Fig. 32.

The end thongs should pass through the loops of thong at (E), which secures the flaps to the sides.

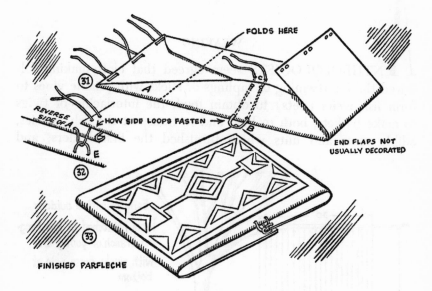

FOLDS HERE

A

REVERSE SIDE OF A
HOW SIDE LOOPS FASTEN →
C
B

END FLAPS NOT USUALLY DECORATED

E

FINISHED PARFLECHE

3. INDIAN WEAVING

WEAVING

ANTHROPOLOGISTS seem agreed that cloth-making followed the intertwining of saplings or sticks with pliable vines to form fish weirs (nets) to obtain food; the interlacing of twigs to make baskets, both to hold and to transport the fish, berries, edible roots and nuts which furnished the first larders; and

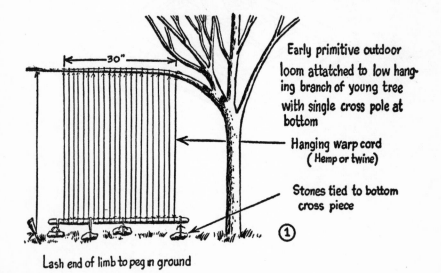

←— 30" —→

Early primitive outdoor loom attatched to low hanging branch of young tree with single cross pole at bottom

Hanging warp cord (Hemp or twine)

Stones tied to bottom cross piece

①

Lash end of limb to peg in ground

forming shapes to barricade the mouth of the family cave shelter against prowling enemies.

From these crude beginnings there developed the one bar loom, a mere pole from which hung strings weighted at the ends with stones to produce tension. The pole was at first probably hung from a tree limb, later supported at each end by crotched sticks stuck into the ground. On this upright loom, the weft or filling thread, wrapped in a ball or around a stick, was inserted laboriously by hand between alternating hanging warp yarns and the web of cloth was gradually produced.

A second type of loom, used for the weaving of silk, consisted of two parallel bars between which the warp was stretched. Among the first improvements were the insertion of two light rods to keep the yarns evenly divided and the addition of two sticks (healds) to which were attached, at equal distances, cord loops. Through these loops were run alternate warp yarns, one stick holding the even-numbered yarns, the other the odd-numbered ones. As the weaver lifted one rod with its attached warps, there was formed a triangular space (shed) through which he threw the weft thread. By lifting first one then the other of the two sticks, alternate groups were raised together saving considerable effort in the insertion of the weft.

Each cross thread was pushed close to the preceding one by a sword-like implement of wood which was later superseded by a comb-like instrument, and as the weaving slowly progressed, a firmly woven fabric evolved.

OUTDOOR LOOMS

Fig. 1 clearly illustrates a primitive outdoor loom attached to a low hanging branch of a young tree. It has a cross-pole suspended at the bottom and held in place by lashing stones to it with leather thong or heavy twine. The tip of the overhanging limb is lashed to a peg in the ground directly beneath.

The warp cords (heavy binding twine or hemp) is strung between the upper tree limb and the bottom cross-pole, which should be about 30″ long and at least one inch thick.

Fig. 2 is a primitive outdoor loom. It is made with two upright poles (D) and a top cross-pole (A), which is lashed to the 2 uprights with leather thong or heavy twine. The frame poles (B and C) that hold the *warp* cords is called the *loom*. The top frame pole (B) is lashed to the top cross-pole with leather thong and the bottom frame pole (C) is held down firmly by lashing the ends to 'Y' pegs in the ground.

How to Weave on a Primitive Loom: In Fig. 2, the *weft*, or

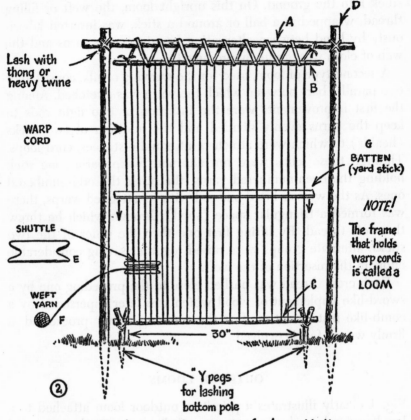

Lash with thong or heavy twine

WARP CORD

SHUTTLE

E

WEFT YARN

F

A

D

B

G BATTEN (yard stick)

NOTE!

The frame that holds warp cords is called a LOOM

C

30"

"Y pegs for lashing bottom pole

② Early primitive loom with 2 cross poles for top and bottom

filling yarn (F) is inserted between the *alternating* hanging *warp* twine with a *shuttle* (E) made out of a thin piece of wood (cigar box wood is good) about five inches long and two inches wide, with notched ends, as shown in illustration (E).

Continue to weave the *weft* yarn in and out between the *warp* cords, back and forth, from left to right. Do not pull the *weft* yarn tightly from one end to the other.

Use a *batten* (G) which can be a yard stick, to press down the *weft* yarn. You can paint the *batten* any desired color to eliminate the inch markings, or decorate it with Indian symbols.

When you come to the end of one piece of *weft* yarn on your *shuttle*, rewind the *shuttle* with new yarn, place the new piece of yarn along-side the old end, and continue weaving.

When you have finished weaving, simply cut the loops around the tree limb and the bottom pole, and tie off the loose ends.

This simple method of weaving will produce a very crude finished product, but will serve as a very easy number-one-step for the young beginner in camp or backyard.

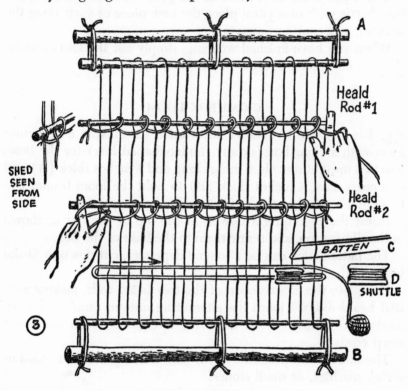

WEAVING WITH TWO HEALD RODS

Fig. 3 illustrates a two-barred (A and B) loom with two *heald rods* (#1 and #2) which are used to pull out the alternating *warp* cords so that the *shuttle* with the *weft* yarn can pass through easily. The space for the *shuttle* to pass through is called the *shed*.

Fasten cord to one end of *heald rod* #1 and loosely loop it under alternating even *warp* cords, and tie at other end. Then fasten cord to one end of *heald rod* #2 and loosely loop the cord under alternating uneven *warp* cords, and tie at other end.

Now you are ready to weave.

Take hold of *heald rod* #1 and pull it towards you, making a *shed*. Pass your *shuttle* (D) through and use your *batten* (C) to push down the *weft* yarn. Now take hold of *heald rod* #2 and pull it towards you, making the second *shed*. Pass your *shuttle* (D) through and repeat the action with the *batten*.

When you come to the end of one piece of *weft* yarn, re-wind the *shuttle* with new yarn; place the new piece of yarn along the old end, and continue weaving.

When you have finished weaving, simply cut the loops around the two end poles, and tie off the loose ends.

CIGAR BOX LOOM

Fig. 4 is a carefully detailed illustration for making a miniature loom with a cigar box (or any similar-shaped box) for the base. Use two upright dowels, 6 inches long and ¾ inches thick (A) and two cross bars, ¼ inches thick (B) to hold the loom frame. Use two dowels ⅛ inches thick (C) to hold the warp cords.

Insert the two upright dowels in the top of the box as shown in the illustration, and screw them to the base of the box.

The batten stick can be a tongue depresser, cut down to fit the width of the loom.

Complete the construction of the two heald rods, making sure that heald rod #1 loops the alternating uneven numbered warp cords, and heald rod #2 loops the alternating even numbered warp cords.

The box can be weighted down with a heavy block of wood or metal, marbles, or small stones.

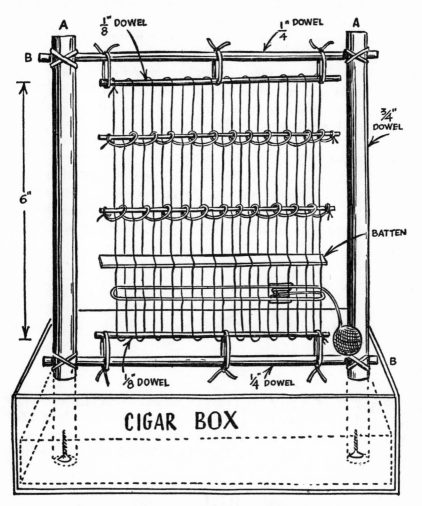

A · B · $\frac{1}{8}$" DOWEL · $\frac{1}{4}$" DOWEL · A · $\frac{3}{4}$" DOWEL · BATTEN · 6" · $\frac{1}{8}$" DOWEL · $\frac{1}{4}$" DOWEL · B

CIGAR BOX

④ Suggested Method for constructing Loom
with cigar box as base. Dotted lines represent
block of wood fitted inside box through which
$\frac{3}{4}$" dowels (A) travel to base of box. Dowels are
secured by screws through base of box.

The word basket is Old English and means a vessel made of vegetable fibers.

Basket-making includes the use of many natural materials such as vegetable fibers, reeds, vines, splints, rushes, grasses, lauhaula, palmetto leaves, long pine needles, straw, and cornhusks.

How to Weave an Indian Basket: Green material is best. There are three methods used in making baskets: weaving, coiling, and braiding. Shown below are the steps in weaving a long, pliable strand called the "WEAVER" over and under a series of spokes or framework.

Step 1. Arrange eight spokes of reeds in a cross. With a sharp knife (X-acto is good), make a slit in the center sections of 4 spokes. Now thread the end of each of the other 4 spokes through the slits (Fig. 5) and pull them through to form a cross.

Step 2. Take a long, well-soaked natural WEAVER of willow or vine, or you can use a commercial weaver. Double it back about 10 inches and wrap the fold around one set of 4 spokes, so that you have a short and a long WEAVER, one on top of the 4

spokes and one underneath, as shown in Fig. 6. Continue weaving over and under the spokes, using both WEAVERS. If the first one starts *under* the first set of spokes, it should go *over* the second set of spokes, under the third, over the fourth, etc. At the same time, the long weaver is going over the first set, under the second, over the third, and under the fourth, as in Fig. 7. Continue for three rows, or until short end is woven in place.

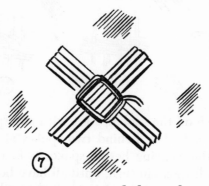

Step 3. Now it is time to spread the spokes evenly, and continue weaving, going under the first and over the second and third spokes, under the fourth, and over the fifth and sixth, as in Fig. 8. Continue until base is the desired size. Be sure to keep the base wet, so that spokes are pliable.

Step 4. Now you are ready to begin turning up the side by turning the spokes up at right angles and continue weaving, as in step 3. Make the basket turn in by pulling the WEAVER tight. Hold spokes at angle to make basket wider.

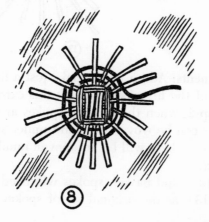

Step 5. To add new WEAVERS, turn end of old WEAVER (A) toward outside of basket, and insert end of new WEAVER (B) about 3 spokes back. Continue with new WEAVER. See Fig. 9.

Step 6. To end WEAVER, cut end of weaver on a slant, with stick end down beside a spoke, as in Fig. 10.

Step 7. To finish off the spokes, start with any spoke and carry it toward inside of basket, behind two spokes at the right, and tuck down into the weaving beside spoke, as in Fig. 11. Repeat this step with each spoke in turn, until all have been tucked into weaving. Press down evenly, and trim off the ends of spokes inside the basket.

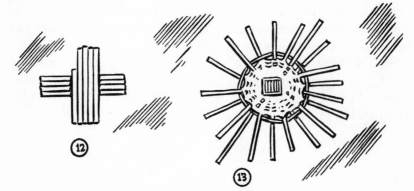

Varied Treatments: Add a ninth spoke just a little longer than half the length of the first spokes. Stick this extra spoke in anywhere, after step 2, when the original spokes are spread evenly. Now the weaver can be woven over and under single spokes for the entire basket as there will be an uneven number of spokes as shown in Fig. 12.

For a larger base and basket, spokes will need to be added to the base (Fig. 13), as the original set of spokes will spread too far for firm weaving. Add a set of pointed spokes between the original spokes, pushing them down hard into the core weaving of step 2. Continue weaving by either method described above.

REFERENCE: This chapter was based freely on Basketry, Chapter III, *Creative Crafts for Campers,* Hammett & Horrocks, Association Press, 291 Broadway, New York, N. Y. Used with permission. This book should be on the shelf of every camp library.

BIBLIOGRAPHY: *Basketry,* Boy Scouts of America. Merit Badge No. 3313.
Basket Pioneering, Orange Judd Publishing Co., New York.
Arts and Crafts with Inexpensive Materials, Girl Scouts of America, New York.
Basketry of the San Carlos Apache, Helen H. Roberts, *Anthropological Papers,* Vol. 31, pt. 2, American Museum of Natural History, New York.
Basketry of the Pimo and Papago, Mary Lois Kissell, *Anthropological Papers,* Vol. 17, pt. 4, American Museum of Natural History, New York.

Excellent Denver Art Museum Leaflets on Basketry:

No. 67, Basketry Construction Technics.

No. 68, Basketry Decoration Technics.

No. 5, Pima Indian Close Coiled Basketry.

No. 17, Hopi Indian Basketry.

No. 64, Apache Indian Coiled Basketry.

Names of Basket Making Materials: (listed in Leaflet No. 83-84, Denver Art Museum, Dept. of Indian Art, Denver, Colorado)

Alder, Bear grass, Bracken fern, Bulrush, Devil's claw, Digger pine, Giant fern, Grape, Grass, Hazel, Maidenhair fern, Marsh grass, Myrtle, Oregon grape, Redbud, Redwood, Rush, Sea blight, Sedge, Spruce, Sumac, Tree yucca, White grass, Willow, Wolf moss, and Yellow pine.

4. ARTS AND DECORATIONS

INDIAN art work included natural forms, such as humans and animals; parts of nature, such as the sun, moon, stars, lightning, thunder, and rain. Other art forms included religious symbols, pictography (the drawing of pictures on stone, bark, bone, and skin, to tell a story, record history, or convey a message), dry painting or sand painting; carving or sculpturing, which was expressed in totem poles, utensils, ornaments and pipes; pottery; metal craft (chiefly copper) implements, ornaments and symbolic objects; decorative elements in weaving, beadwork, quillwork, and basketry. Tattooing and coloring the human body was also done.

INDIAN DYES AND PAINTS

The North American Indian used a large number of plant stems, leaves, roots, nuts, seeds, and inner bark to make dyes, stains, and some paints. They also employed the use of ground-up colored rocks and stones, ochers (earthy varieties of iron ore), limestones, iron-bearing minerals, ores, gypsum, charcoal, and soot.

Almost any plant will produce some kind of color. Just recall all the things that have stained your fingers!

The Denver Art Museum, Department of Indian Art, has a very complete listing of Indian dyes in their leaflets, Nos. 63 and 71. Curator Frederic H. Douglas states that before the introduction of various types of dyes by Europeans and Americans, the Indians used a number of plants as sources for dyes, stains, and paints, in a wide range of colors. He goes on to say that the introduction of commercial dyes has resulted in the abandonment of many of these dyes, though some have survived and others have been introduced in recent years. He tells us that this is particularly true of the Navahos, who, thanks to the revival of their weaving through the efforts of interested whites, are today using many more vegetable dyes than they did under aboriginal conditions.

Ingredients You Can Use for Making Indian Dyes:

Yellow: The stems and roots of the wild barberry, sassafras bark, the flowers and stems of the goldenrod, the bark of the speckled alder, or the roots of the Oregon grape.

Black: The bark of the mountain mahogany or black walnut root.

Brown: Leaves, hulls, and whole nut of the wild black walnut or butternut bark.

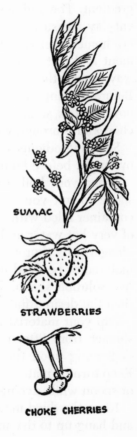

SUMAC

STRAWBERRIES

CHOKE CHERRIES

Orange: Root of the bloodroot.

Blue: The flowers of the blue larkspur.

Green: Green leaves. Some desert Indians obtained green from the pricklypear. Algae growing in stagnant pools can be freshly rubbed into wood and leather for a green effect.

Red: Pokeberries, choke cherries, elderberries, sumac berries, and strawberries.

Mordants, "Mixing" Chemicals: Natural dyes are much softer than commercial dyes and do not hold their color unless the material to be dyed is treated with a mordant or "mixing" chemical to hold and set the colors. For silk or wool, the mordant is made with water and alum (one ounce of alum to a gallon of water) plus one-quarter ounce of cream of tartar. For cotton, linen, or rayon, one-quarter ounce of plain washing soda should be added to the alum and water solution. The material should be soaked for about one hour in the mordant solution, then well rinsed before dyeing.

Preparing Indian Dyes: The time for boiling your dyes varies from thirty minutes to six hours, depending upon the ingredient. The Indians did not use present-day measuring utensils of the modern homemaker! You will have to experiment and test as you go along. By the way, wool is the best material for dyeing. Before boiling, be sure to crush the flower petals, scrape and crush the stems, chop and thoroughly clean the roots.

Soak ingredients for several hours or overnight before boiling.

When your boiled dye has reached a shade to suit you, strain it into a large container filled with at least four gallons of very hot water and add a little salt or vinegar. Mix thoroughly before dipping material to be dyed in the solution. The dye solution should be darker in color than the desired finished shade.

Dip your material in the dye vat and simmer from fifteen to thirty minutes, depending upon the shade you desire. Keep turning material with wooden stick or spoon while dyeing.

Rinse the dyed material in cold water and hang up to dry in a shady place.

LARKSPUR

BLACK WALNUT

PRICKLY PEAR

BLOODROOT

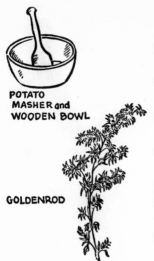

POTATO
MASHER and
WOODEN BOWL

GOLDENROD

Ingredients for Making Indian Paints:
White: Ground-up white limestone or gypsum.
Red: Ground-up red limestone or ocher.
Yellow: Ground-up yellow limestone or ocher.
Black: Powdered charcoal or coal or soot.
Mixer: Indians mixed the powdered or ground-up ingredients with animal fat or grease and heated the mixture. Some tribes used hoof glue. Face paint was mixed with grease or saliva.

Substitute Materials: There are many kinds of commercial dyes on the market. Each package gives complete directions for dyeing materials. A great variety of paints are available. We recommend Grumbacher oil tube paints, Prang's textile colors or Grumbacher tempera colors in powder form. This last type of color is water soluble and must be lacquer or crylon sprayed after applying.

INDIAN COLOR MEANINGS

Colors in Indian designs and symbols had a particular meaning in different tribes. Here is a partial list of colors and their meanings:
Red: Wound, sunset, thunder, blood, earth, south.
White: Winter, death, east.
Blue: Sky, day, water, west.
Black: Night, underworld.
Yellow: Sunlight, day, east, dawn, north.
Green: Growing things, earth, summer, west.

REFERENCES AND BIBLIOGRAPHY: Dyeing with Natural Dyes, page 328, *Creative Crafts for Campers*, Hammett and Horrocks, Association Press, 291 Broadway, New York, N. Y.
Leaflets 43 & 44, 56, 63, 71, 89, 96 & 97. Denver Art Museum, Department of Indian Art, 1300 Logan Street, Denver, Colorado.
Native Dyes, page 68, *Yellowstone's Bannock Indian Trails*, Wayne

F. Replogle, Yellowstone Interpretive Series No. 6, Yellowstone National Park, Wyoming.

Dyes, *Bulletin 30*, page 408, Bureau of American Ethnology, Washington, D. C.

Book of Arts and Crafts, Ickis and Esh, Association Press, 291 Broadway, New York, N. Y.

Plates 1 and 2 include some designs of the Plains Indians. Plate 3 shows some Woodland Indian designs. Some very meaningful symbols are outlined on Plate 4. Some suggested motifs from the Plains and Woodland tribes are detailed on Plates 5 and 6.

Reference: Indian Leaflet Series No. 61, Symbolism in Indian Art and the Difficulties of its Interpretation, Denver Art Museum, Denver, Colo.

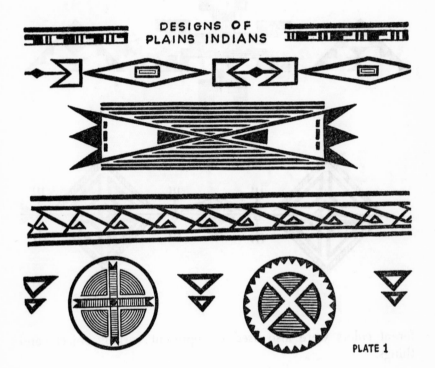

DESIGNS OF PLAINS INDIANS

PLATE 1

SYMBOL—A symbol is something that represents something else, not by exact resemblance, but by suggestion or association in thought. A good example is the cross, the symbol of Christianity, or the $ mark, symbol for dollars.

Symbols were used by Indians to tell a story, preserve the history of the tribe; they were placed on religious or ceremonial objects or used on totem poles to represent the family history. Dif-

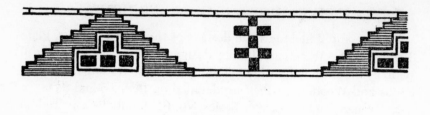

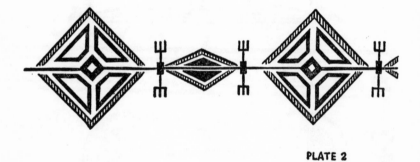

PLATE 2

ferent colors were also used to represent various objects and things.

DESIGN—The combination of details that make up a work of art.

All Indian designs do not necessarily have a "meaning." They were often created by the imagination of the artist in a desire to have his creation pleasing to the eye.

MOTIF—A distinctive feature or element of a design.

A good example would be the use of an arrowhead as the major motif in a complete design.

WOODLAND DESIGNS

DELAWARE BORDER

FROM OJIBWAY BEADWORK

OJIBWAY (EASTERN)

EASTERN   ALGONKIAN

NORTHEASTERN   PLATE 3

SYMBOLS *and their meaning*

THUNDERBIRD
Sacred Bearer of Happiness

BEAR TRACK
Good Omen

MAN
Human Life

BUTTERFLY
Everlasting Life

CROSSED ARROWS
Friendship

RAIN CLOUDS
Good Prospects

ARROW
Protection

DAYS and NIGHTS
Time

ARROWHEAD
Alertness

MEDICINE MAN'S EYE
Wise, Watchful

4 AGES
Infancy, Youth Middle & Old Age

HOGAN
Permanent Home

CACTUS FLOWER
Courtship

BIG MOUNTAIN
Abundance

HORSE
Journey

WARDING OFF EVIL SPIRITS

SUN RAYS
Constancy

PATHS CROSSING

SUN SYMBOLS
Happiness

PLATE 4

RATTLESNAKE JAW
Strength

Frederic H. Douglas, Curator, Denver Art Museum, makes an excellent summary in Symbolism in Indian Art and the Difficulties of its Interpretation, Leaflet 61, when he states, "The Indian tribes have a number of groups of design elements, to which names are usually given for convenience only, the names having no connection with symbolic practices. These elements may be used for decoration or to express several kinds of ideas through symbolism. The wish of the individual artist determines for which of these two purposes any design is made, and its meaning if it be symbolic. Accurate interpretation is impossible unless the actual maker explains each design, though quite good guesses may be sometimes made by experts. An extremely small number of symbols are universally recognized in some individual tribes.

"As far as the average person who looks at objects of Indian manufacture is concerned, it is impossible to recognize or interpret Indian designs as symbols."

SUGGESTED MOTIFS FROM THE
PLAINS and WOODLAND TRIBES

PLATE 5

PLATE 6

5. MUSIC AND MUSICAL INSTRUMENTS

MUSIC and rhythm were very important in the Indian's life. Most people think of Indian music as the beating of a tom-tom, the shaking of rattles, and barbaric discords. This is not true. Indian music is harmonious, rhythmic, and appealing. The Indian considers the rhythm of the white man's music rather dull and uninteresting because it is so simple in comparison to theirs.

If a present-day orchestra conductor would gather together a group of Indian musicians, he could marshall players for the string, wind, and percussion sections. In the string section he could use a musical bow, somewhat like the jew's harp, played by the Maidu tribe of California. It was usually played by the young men when serenading their sweethearts in the quiet of the night. The Apache Indian would play a fiddle made from the hollow stem of the agave ore aloe with wooden disks inserted in the ends. One or two horsehair strings are stretched along the tube over a bridge. One end of the tube is pressed against the player's body, while a short, deeply curved bow of wood and horsehair is drawn over the strings. Hopi flutes, somewhat like the primitive flageolet, would be played in the wind section. The Hupa bone pan-pipes could be used for the cry of birds or animals.

In the percussion section we would have a great variety of

drums, including the small hand drum, the large two-headed drum, the water drum, the hung drum, the clay bowl drum, the wooden bowl drum, and, of course, the modern bass drum, now used by many present-day tribes. We would also include the rattle, made of turtle shells, cow horns, bark, gourds, and stiff leather; and we would employ the notched resonator, a stick or long bone on which are cut a series of deep grooves, along which a piece of smooth stick or bone is vigorously rubbed up and down.

For the reader seriously interested in the music and musical instruments of the Indian, we recommend the following partial list of references and bibliographies:

REFERENCES AND BIBLIOGRAPHIES: Indian Musical and Noise-Making Instruments, Leaflet No. 29, *Indian Leaflet Series,* Department of Indian Art, Denver Art Museum, Denver, Colorado.

The American Indian and Their Music, Frances Densmore, The Women's Press, New York, N. Y.

Indian Story and Song, Alice C. Fletcher, Small Maynard & Co., Boston, Mass.

Article on Musical Instruments, Fletcher, *Bulletin No. 30,* page 960, Bureau of American Ethnology, Washington, D. C.

HOW TO MAKE AN INDIAN DRUM

Figs. 1 through 5 show five easy steps in making a drum out of a discarded nail keg. First, remove the bottom of the keg. Sandpaper the staves smooth with coarse sandpaper and paint the keg with two coats of white house paint. Fig. 2 shows you how to paint the drum with Indian designs (Chapter 4, Indian Arts and Decorations) making sure to use bright colors. Regular house paint will do, or you can use enamel.

For the drum heads, secure two fresh calf skins from a butcher, slaughter house, or leather supply house. Make sure that it is not tanned or dried. Stretch the drum head over the ends of the keg, as shown in Fig. 4, and lace the two pieces together, as illustrated in Fig. 5. You can use an old inner tube for substitute drum heads.

A discarded nail keg with bottom removed painted with 2 coats of white is basis for drum.

(1)

Paint areas shaded in diagonal lines RED and 2 center steel bands in BLUE

(2)

If hide is not available an old inner tube cut about 4" larger in circumference than keg will make a fine drum

Holes punched about 2" apart and 1" in from edge are for heavy twine or thongs

(3)

Stretch rubber discs over ends of keg and tie down with heavy thong

(4)

Lace heavy thong back and forth between top & bottom as shown. Draw tighter (careful not to cut through holes) until full vibrant tone is produced.

(5)

This same type drum in miniature can be made from discarded coffee can.

BEATER

Wrap cord around notch forming ball

Stretch piece of cloth over ball then tie with cord

TIES IN CENTER OF BOTTOM

B

(CHEESE BOX)

C

6

HANDLES NOTCHED FOR THONGS

Grooved cross pieces

HUNG DRUM 7

Made from large cheese box and walking canes

← inset shows screw to fasten cane to base

WOODEN SALAD BOWL DRUM

THONGS TIED BOTTOM CENTER

9

8 WATER DRUM

Made from hollowed out log with hole near bottom for draining. Varying level of water produces different tones.

A

Fig. 6 is a tambourine type of hand drum. The frame (C) can be made from the lid of a cheese box. Lace the drum head to the frame, as shown in (B), with leather thong.

Fig. 7 is a hanging drum, which can be made with a large cheese box lid for the frame of the drum. Lace the drum head to the frame, as shown in Fig. 6. Suspend it with leather thong to four upright walking canes or wooden stakes, which have been screwed to the bottom cross-boards with long, thin screws and braced with short right-angle sticks of wood, as detailed in illustration.

Decorate your drum with a border of fringed bright-colored cloth, leather or plastic fringe, and paint Indian designs on the drum head. Paint the canes or uprights with bright colored oil or enamel paints.

Fig. 8 is a water drum made from a hollowed out log, with a bung hole near the bottom for filling and draining. Varying level of water will produce different tones.

Fig. 9 is a wooden salad bowl drum. Secure the drum head to the bowl, as indicated in illustration A.

A tin can (coffee, shortening, etc.) tom tom is very simple to make. Remove the lid, use inner tubing for the drum heads and lace them together with thong, shoe string, or twine. Paint the sides and top drum head with Indian designs.

Your drum stick can be a tree branch about 12 inches long. Wrap cord around the notched end, forming a ball. Stretch a small piece of soft leather or cloth over the ball and tie with thong or cord, as illustrated.

BIBLIOGRAPHY: Excellent descriptions and illustrations of Indian drums can be found in *The Golden Book of Indian Crafts and Lore*, W. B. Hunt, Simon & Schuster, New York, N. Y.

Indian Materials You Can Use: Turtle shells, bark, leather, cow horn, gourds, wood, and clay.

Substitute Materials: Small tin can or small cardboard or wooden boxes.

Tools and Equipment You Will Need: Hammer, small nails, scissors, knife; piece of broom handle or dowel rod for rattle handles; drill and bit to make holes for turtle shell and bark rattles; coping saw for cutting cow horn rattles; glue for gourd rattle top; paint brushes.

Indian Decorations: Feathers, horsehair; vegetable or root dyes.

Substitute Decorations: Narrow strips of bright colored cloth or ribbon, yarn tassels, oil paints, enamels, or lacquers.

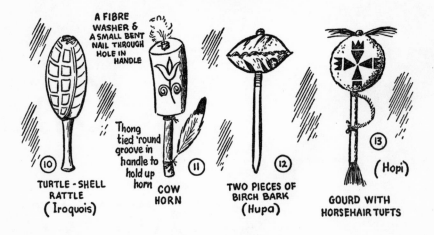

A FIBRE WASHER & A SMALL BENT NAIL THROUGH HOLE IN HANDLE

Thong tied 'round groove in handle to hold up horn

TURTLE-SHELL RATTLE (Iroquois) — ⑩

COW HORN — ⑪

TWO PIECES OF BIRCH BARK (Hupa) — ⑫

GOURD WITH HORSEHAIR TUFTS (Hopi) — ⑬

Instructions for Making Rattles: Fig. 10 is a turtle rattle. The turtle shells and the two pieces of bark can be laced together by drilling small holes around the edges for the "in-and-out" lacing. Use a piece of broom handle or dowel rod for the handle; insert it and secure it to the top of the rattle, as illustrated.

Fig. 11 is a cow horn rattle. It can be secured with leather thong tied around the handle and a small nail with fiber washer at the top.

Fig. 12 is a birch bark rattle laced together with leather thong.

Fig. 13 is a gourd rattle, decorated with horsehair tufts.

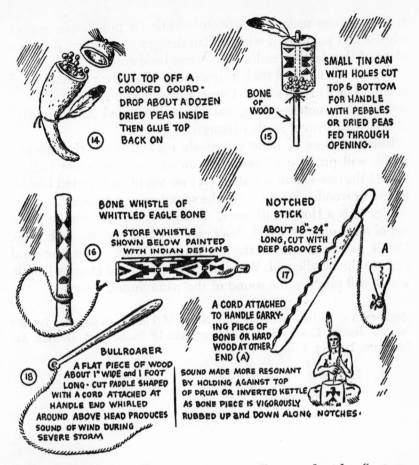

CUT TOP OFF A CROOKED GOURD · DROP ABOUT A DOZEN DRIED PEAS INSIDE THEN GLUE TOP BACK ON

(14)

BONE or WOOD →

(15)

SMALL TIN CAN WITH HOLES CUT TOP & BOTTOM FOR HANDLE WITH PEBBLES OR DRIED PEAS FED THROUGH OPENING.

BONE WHISTLE OF WHITTLED EAGLE BONE

A STORE WHISTLE SHOWN BELOW PAINTED WITH INDIAN DESIGNS

(16)

NOTCHED STICK

ABOUT 18"-24" LONG, CUT WITH DEEP GROOVES

(17)

A

A CORD ATTACHED TO HANDLE CARRY-ING PIECE OF BONE OR HARD WOOD AT OTHER END (A)

BULLROARER

(18)

A FLAT PIECE OF WOOD ABOUT 1" WIDE and 1 FOOT LONG · CUT PADDLE SHAPED WITH A CORD ATTACHED AT HANDLE END WHIRLED AROUND ABOVE HEAD PRODUCES SOUND OF WIND DURING SEVERE STORM

SOUND MADE MORE RESONANT BY HOLDING AGAINST TOP OF DRUM OR INVERTED KETTLE AS BONE PIECE IS VIGOROUSLY RUBBED UP and DOWN ALONG NOTCHES·

Fig. 14 shows you how to cut the top off a gourd with a "nature-formed" handle and drop in a dozen or so of dried peas or small pebbles, and glue the top back on.

Fig. 15 is a rattle made out of a small tin can or cardboard container, showing the details of inserting and attaching the broom stick or dowel rod handle.

Instructions for Decorating Your Rattle: You can paint the rattle with Indian designs (Chapter 4, Indian Arts and Decorations) or you can stamp the designs on the tin can with large nail and hammer. You can also cover the rattle with thin leather, plastic, or fur. Attach narrow strips of colored cloth, ribbon, small feathers, horsehair, bits of metal, and large beads.

Fig. 16 is an Indian bone whistle. Since it is rather difficult to make, you can make a substitute whistle by purchasing a store whistle and painting it with Indian designs or covering it with a piece of thin leather and adding some beadwork.

Fig. 17 is a notched stick or resonator. Use a stick of hard wood about 18 or 24 inches long. Carve a handle at one end and cut a series of deep notches along one side, as illustrated. Attach a piece of bone to a strip of leather thong.

Rub the piece of bone vigorously up and down the notches, which will produce a "morache" sound. Sometimes the Indians placed the one end of the stick (A) on top of an inverted basket, gourd, or wooden bowl to give the sound more resonance.

Fig. 18 is a Hopi "bullroarer," a noise-maker that can be made out of a flat piece of wood about one foot long and one inch wide. Cut it paddle shaped. Attach a leather thong, about one yard long, to the handle end. Whirl it above your head at arms-length, and it will produce the sound of the wind during a storm.

REFERENCES: Indian Musical and Noise-Making Instruments, Leaflet No. 29, *Indian Leaflet Series,* Department of Indian Art, Denver Art Museum, Denver, Colo.

6. COMMUNICATION AND RECORD-KEEPING

INDIAN SIGNALS AND SIGNS

THE Indian used a wide range of signals including:

Smoke Signals for Daytime: Smoke signals were made on high elevations of land. Sometimes they could be seen at a distance of from twenty to fifty miles. By varying the number of smoke columns, different meanings were conveyed. Sometimes the Indian simply built a small fire which was not allowed to blaze, then

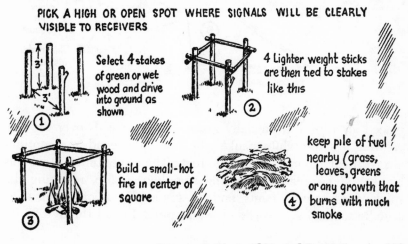

PICK A HIGH OR OPEN SPOT WHERE SIGNALS WILL BE CLEARLY VISIBLE TO RECEIVERS

① Select 4 stakes of green or wet wood and drive into ground as shown

② 4 Lighter weight sticks are then tied to stakes like this

③ Build a small-hot fire in center of square

④ keep pile of fuel nearby (grass, leaves, greens or any growth that burns with much smoke

← 7"to 8" →

HOLE

12"

⑤

SMOKE CLOTH
Discarded piece
of burlap or
canvas

SIGNAL CLOTH
WET BOTH cloths
so they won't burn

← 4'to5' →

STONES

⑥

Small stake

DRAFT

Lay smoke cloth over
fire securing it as
shown

... A quick swing upward
of the SIGNAL CLOTH

One second later

Place quantity of moist
fuel on fire ... Place damp
SIGNAL CLOTH over
SMOKE CLOTH ... Waiting
about 30 seconds

⑦

BEATER
Long piece
of brush

⑧

strike
smoke
cloth
with
beater

This creates
distinct
signals

placed an armful of partially green grass or weeds over the fire,
creating a dense white smoke which would ascend in a continu-
ous vertical column for many feet. Then the Indian took his
blanket and spread it over the smouldering fire, retaining the
smoke for a few moments, and he was ready to convey his message by sending up a series of smoke puffs. Figs. 1 through 8.

Fire Signals for Night: Building a series of fires on a high elevation, the Indian could convey messages such as one fire for calling attention, two fires to indicate that all is well, three fires as a call for help, four fires meaning to come to the village, etc. Sometimes the Indians would "blink" the fire (Fig. 10).

Blanket Signals: The Plains Indians used a blanket to transmit signals and conversations from high elevations. The tribal scout could inform his village that he had sighted a herd of buffalo or the enemy. Secret signals were made by tossing or waving the blanket in a certain manner (Fig. 9).

Drums: Certain secret beats on the drum would convey messages from one village to another.

BLANKET SIGNALS

SMALL FIRES FOR NIGHT SIGNALS

1 Fire { ATTENTION!

2 Fires { ALL IS WELL!

3 Fires { CALL FOR HELP!

4 Fires { COME TO POW WOW!

REFERENCES AND BIBLIOGRAPHY FOR INDIAN SIGNALS: From: "*Social Organization and Social Usages of the Indians of the Creek Confederacy*" by John R. Swanton, published in the Forty-second Annual Report of the Bureau of American Ethnology.

"*Antiquities of the Upper Verde River and Walnut Creek Valleys, Arizona*" by Jesse Walter Fewkes, published in the Twenty-eighth Annual Report of the Bureau of American Ethnology.

From: article on Signals in Bureau of American Ethnology *Bulletin 30, "Handbook of American Indians."*

Fremont's First and Second Expeditions, 1842–3–4, *Ex. Doc., 28th Congress, 2nd Session*, Senate, Washington, 1845, page 407, under the title of *TINNEAN, (Apache I)*.

The Book of American Indians, Ralph B. Raphael, Fawcett Book.

Cry of the Thunderbird, Charles Hamilton, The Macmillan Co., New York, N. Y.

THIS WAY ➡

LONG DISTANCE

⬅ THIS WAY

SHORT DISTANCE

HELP

Red

WAR TRAIL

GASH IN TREE BARK
INDICATED POOR
HUNTING GROUND

CUT STRIP IN BARK
INDICATED
SICKNESS IN TRIBE

TRAIL BEGINS

TURN TO THE
RIGHT

TURN TO THE
LEFT

In an unknown area
which is stony, a group
forming an arrow head
was frequently used

If travelling over
barren or desert
areas arrows were
marked on ground
with sharp stick.

Grassy lands where
marked with clumps
tied together by strands
of taller grass indicated route.

⑪

Trail Signs: Twigs and small sticks were stuck in the ground to indicate trail directions, distance, call for help, etc. Sometimes messages were conveyed by bending tree limbs and twigs and cutting marks in the bark of trees. Fig. 11.

3 sticks hung in a bundle from a tree, crossbar or post means "quicksand or deep mud nearby". Added to this was a clean-cut arrow in tree nearest the area directing you there

"Deep holes" or possible "Cave Ins" were usually marked with a single stick hanging from a crossbar

A

A frame of posts with a stone hung from top cross bar means "All nearby water is bad or poisonous for drinking"

Diagram (A) has same meaning but would wash away

This arrangement means "Dangerous Animals Nearby"

Fast riding horsemen were warned to slow down for "Cliff or Sharp Drop-Off Ahead" through this sign.

The 3 signal methods illustrated above mean— "HELP NEEDED··· THIS WAY"

Warning Signs: Small rocks and stones were placed in definite formations to show the trail, danger, etc. See Fig. 12.

PICTOGRAPHY

Making Your Own
"WINTER COUNTER"

← For inside use

Secure 4 Straight Poles (preferably White Birch)
about 1" to 2" in diameter.

If actual hide is not available a piece of heavy
corrugated cardboard from a mattress covering will
be suitable. Cut in irregular shape to imitate hide.

Grommets should be inserted about 1½" from edges
and about every foot through which thong will be fed
for looping over outside poles.

⑬ Make up your own "Pictograph" story and paint on
hide or cardboard. See text for full details.

PICTOGRAPHY

The Indians used pictography (picture-writing) to tell a story, to record the events that happened in past years, important ceremonials, and treaties. These calendars or "winter-counts," (each year is a "winter") were painted on deer, antelope, or buffalo hides. The Dakota calendars have a picture for each year's winter, while those of the Kiowa use month, summer, and winter symbols.

HOW TO MAKE A "WINTER-COUNTER"

Indian Materials You Can Use: Smooth-surfaced hide, four straight, stout poles, long enough to frame your hide (white birch is excellent), and enough leather thong or heavy twine for lashing the poles and lacing the hide to the frame.

Substitute Materials: A good looking imitation animal hide can be made out of a heavy corrugated cardboard mattress packing case. Cut it in the shape of a hide, as shown on Fig. 13.

Tools and Equipment You Will Need: Hand ax, enough leather thong to lash the poles and lace the hide, sharp knife or shears, paint brushes, and enough ¼" grommets to go around the edging of the hide, about one foot apart. Grommets are not Indian, but *should* be used to prevent the tearing of the hide.

Indian Decorations: Vegetable, berry, or root dyes.

Substitute Decorations: Crayons, oil paints, lacquers, water or poster paints.

Instructions for Making "Winter-Counter": Refer to Fig. 13. Secure four straight poles (white birch is excellent) about one or two inches thick. Fasten the four corners with thong, making sure to wet it before lashing. Stamp the edgings of the hide with grommets (metal eyelets) about one foot apart, to prevent tearing it when laced to the frame.

The two upright poles can be painted at the bottom ends for standing it outdoors, or you may prefer to use a simple crossboard stand for indoor use, as shown in the illustration.

Instructions for Decorating "Winter-Counter": Make up your own pictograph story and paint it on the hide; refer to Fig. 14.

INDIAN PICTURE WRITING

Below

Brothers

Come

Day

Deer

Eat

Fear

Grass

Hear

Bear Alive

Bear Dead

Beaver

Cloud

Plenty Corn

Whooping Cough

Calumet Dance

Death

Cactus

Canyon

Dead

Earth Lodge

Geese

Stone Hammer

House

Meteor

Old

Otter

Strong

Thunderbird

Travois

Turtle

Walk

War

⑭

Another form of Indian picture writing was petroglyphs, which means scratching, chipping or chiseling Indian symbols on large boulders, sides of cliffs, and in caves. Sometimes the markings were filled in with Indian dyes and paints.

Dr. Dorothy Cross, New Jersey State Museum anthropological adviser, tells us that museums are sometimes confronted by excited visitors who bring them bits of stone incised with Indian markings, only to discover after much time and study, that they are the work of modern-day "eager beavers," playing Indian. Don't scatter your marked stones to the four winds. Keep them in your private collection!

TOTEM POLES

"And they painted on the grave-posts
Each his own ancestral totem,
Each the symbol of his household;
Figures of the bear and reindeer,
Of the turtle, crane and beaver,
Each inverted as a token
That the owner was departed."
—Longfellow

To the Indians of the northwest coast, the totem pole with its fantastic carvings meant many things, including a memorial to the dead, a record of the family, clan or tribe, and legends.

The noted anthropologist, F. H. Douglas, tells us that the word "totem" means "his brother-sister kin"; that is, the group of brothers and sisters born to one mother, and persons adopted into such a group.

Some totem pole designs were animal figures, each animal symbolizing a family crest or story.

Some totem poles were as tall as seventy feet and stood in front of the rows of houses. Some were attached to the front of the house and short ones were set inside the houses.

Making a totem pole was an expensive and difficult job. A red cedar tree was cut down, dragged to the sea, and towed to the village. It was placed on convenient supports for the carver. Sometimes the back of the pole was hollowed out to make it easier to handle.

The poles were erected by placing the butt end in a pit with one sloping side and then raised upright by pushing and pulling with poles and ropes.

 The Northwest Coast Indians were producers of large quantities of wood carvings, among the most ambitious of which were Totem Poles.

The totem began as a stout cedar pole standing at the corners of their houses. Later a taller single pole was erected directly in front of the house.

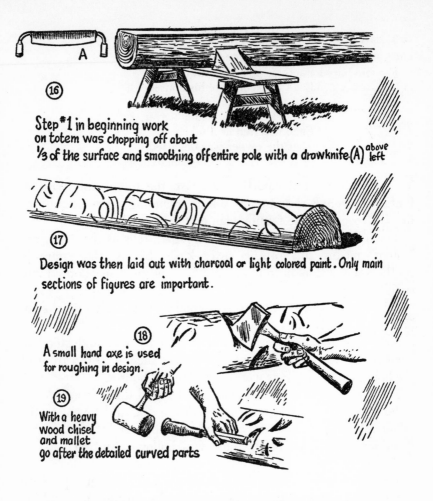

Step #1 in beginning work
on totem was chopping off about
⅓ of the surface and smoothing off entire pole with a drawknife.(A) above left

Design was then laid out with charcoal or light colored paint. Only main
, sections of figures are important.

A small hand axe is used
for roughing in design.

With a heavy
wood chisel
and mallet
go after the detailed curved parts

HOW TO MAKE LARGE, SMALL, AND MINIATURE TOTEM POLES

Indian Materials You Can Use: Select your pole very carefully for the large totem pole. Choose a soft wood with as few knots as possible, unless such knots lend themselves well to a certain design or figure. The best wood for a large totem pole is red cedar. Others are spruce, soft pine, willow, cottonwood, basswood, aspen, white pine, hemlock, and tulip. Green woods will carve more easily than dry.

You can use soft pine or balsa wood for miniature totem poles.

Substitute Materials: For the small totem poles, you can substitute nail kegs, cardboard oatmeal boxes, shortening cans, coffee cans, and balsa wood.

For the paper mache pole, you can use furnace pipe or linoleum shipping tubes.

Tools and Equipment You Will Need: For the large totem pole, you will need lumberman's crayon, wooden mallet; half inch, one inch, and one and a half inch chisels, hand ax; one inch and one and a half inch gouges, and a two-handled draw knife. For the small and miniature totem poles you will need a coping saw, pencil, and sharp knife.

Indian Decorations: The large totem poles were painted and unpainted. Some of the old poles were decorated with vegetable and root dyes. The same holds true for the smaller poles.

Substitute Decorations: After the coming of the white man, the Indians adopted the use of bright paints.

Making the Large Totem Pole: Refer to Figs. 16-20. Place your pole on two saw horses, first chopping off a portion of the back of the pole to make it rest firmly on the saw horses, as shown in Fig. 16. Smooth off the other portion of the pole with a two-handled draw knife. Now choose your designs and outline the figures on the pole with lumberman's crayon, as shown in Fig. 17.

Then chop and carve out the figures, as shown in Figs. 18-19-20.

You can leave it unpainted or you can paint it with bright colored oil paints or enamel. Be sure to use a good grade to withstand the weather.

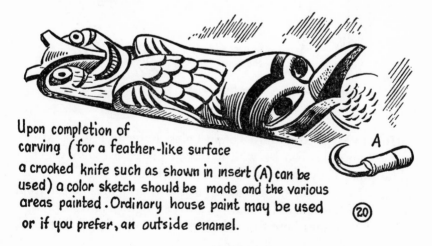

Upon completion of carving (for a feather-like surface a crooked knife such as shown in insert (A) can be used) a color sketch should be made and the various areas painted. Ordinary house paint may be used or if you prefer, an outside enamel.

Lead Pencil and Small Branch Totem Poles: Fig. 21 shows you how the illustrator made an attractive totem pole out of a large pencil.

Fig. 22 shows how the illustrator carved a totem pole from a small piece of a tree branch and applied a rubber stamp with initials on the bottom.

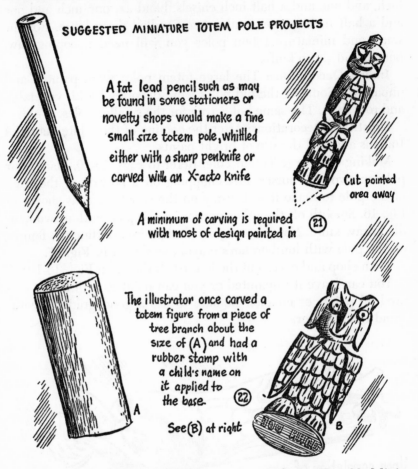

SUGGESTED MINIATURE TOTEM POLE PROJECTS

A fat lead pencil such as may be found in some stationers or novelty shops would make a fine small size totem pole, whittled either with a sharp penknife or carved with an X-acto knife

A minimum of carving is required with most of design painted in ㉑

Cut pointed area away

The illustrator once carved a totem figure from a piece of tree branch about the size of (A) and had a rubber stamp with a child's name on it applied to the base. ㉒

See (B) at right

A

B

How to Make Miniature Totem Poles: Refer to Fig. 23. Miniature totem poles can be whittled from pieces of balsa wood or white pine. They can be three, five, or ten inches high.

Fig. 23A and 23B show how to outline your figures on the front and side of the squared wood. Divide your figures into sections.

Fig. 23C shows how the pole begins to take shape. The back

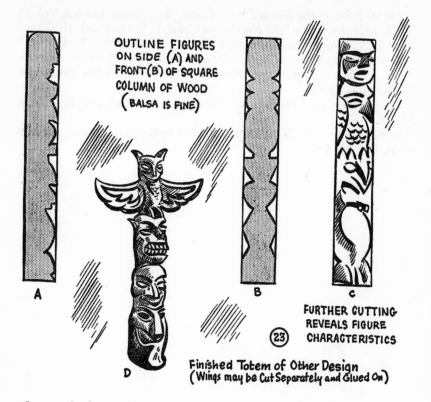

OUTLINE FIGURES ON SIDE (A) AND FRONT (B) OF SQUARE COLUMN OF WOOD (BALSA IS FINE)

FURTHER CUTTING REVEALS FIGURE CHARACTERISTICS

(23)

Finished Totem of Other Design (Wings may be Cut Separately and Glued On)

side can be perfectly flat, if desired, or you may wish to carve clear around the pole.

Fig. 23D shows you a completed totem of different design.

Decorating Your Miniature Totem Pole: You can use water colors, oil paints, or dyes, applied with a small pointed paint brush. Outline the figures with black and use bright contrasting colors.

A 9-inch-high, molded, solid plastic totem pole kit, "Paint-A-Pole," ready to be painted, has recently been placed on the market by the Cleveland Crafts Co. It contains two different totem poles with a lock device, enabling one to put them together to form one solid totem pole.

References and Bibliography for Totem Poles: United States National Museum, Washington, D. C.

The Coast Indians of Southern Alaska and Northern British Columbia, A. P. Niblack, American Museum of Natural History, New York.

Totem Poles of the North Pacific Coast, H. I. Smith. Journal, Vol. 11, No. 3, 1911, *Indians of the Northwest Coast*, P. E. Goddard. Handbook No. 10, 1924, American Museum of Natural History, New York.

Totem Poles; A Recent Native Art of the Northwest Coast of America, C. M. Barbeau, Report, pp. 559-570, 1931, Smithsonian Institution, Washington, D. C.

Monuments in Cedar, E. L. Keithahn. 1945, Roy Anderson, Ketchikan, Alaska.

Indian Leaflet No. 79-80, Department of Indian Art, Denver Art Museum, Denver, Colo.

Some Indians, the Winnebagos particularly, kept a record of months and years on a Calendar Stick, which were handed down from generation to generation.

Fig. 24 shows how the stick had notches on the flat side for the moons or months and those on the sides recorded the "winters" or years. Sometimes notches were cut to show the ages of the members in the family.

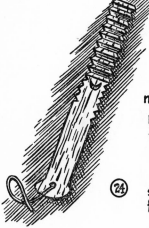

WINNEBAGO CALENDAR STICK

Notches on face of stick show moons, or months. The side notches represent years. At the sound of the first thunder of the season the first yearly notch was usually cut.

Four or even six-sided sticks were sometimes used, one side being for each family member.

(24)

1 DAY • A SUN   Travels from horizon to horizon

1 NIGHT • A Sleep

1 MONTH • A MOON

1 YEAR • A WINTER or GREAT SUN

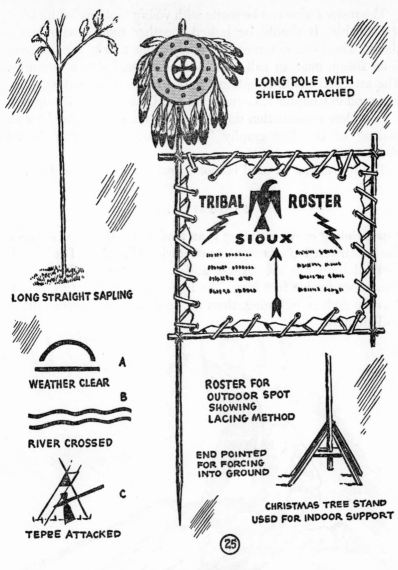

LONG POLE WITH SHIELD ATTACHED

LONG STRAIGHT SAPLING

TRIBAL ROSTER

SIOUX

WEATHER CLEAR A

RIVER CROSSED B

TEPEE ATTACKED C

ROSTER FOR OUTDOOR SPOT SHOWING LACING METHOD

END POINTED FOR FORCING INTO GROUND

CHRISTMAS TREE STAND USED FOR INDOOR SUPPORT

25

TRIBAL ROSTER
(name-recorder)

A very handsome Tribal Roster or "name-recorder," is shown in Fig. 25. The Father and Son Y-Indian Guides Tallykeeper, and the Boy Scout Order of the Arrow use it to keep a record of their tribal members.

The roster frame can be made with young saplings, white birch, if available. It should be lashed together tightly with leather thong. The hide, cut roughly to resemble a pelt, can be made from sheep, goat, or calf skin. A sand-colored skin is preferred. The attached shield is optional and directions for making it can be found in Chapter 7, Ceremonial and Council Ring Equipment.

Complete construction details are the same as outlined for the making of the Pictography "Winter-Counter," earlier in this chapter.

The Roster can be used indoors, outdoors, or hung on the wall.

SANDPAINTING

Sandpainting or dry-painting is an ancient art that the Indians of the Southwest have known for centuries (Fig. 26). The Navaho sandpaintings are the largest and most complicated. They are sometimes twelve feet long. The figures on sandpainting may be Navaho gods of lightning, thunder, sunbeams, mountains, plants, and animals.

To make a sandpainting, the men cover the floor of a hogan with clean white sand. The sand is between two and three inches deep. They smooth it down with wooden blocks. Then they bring in small pouches of colored sand—yellow, red, black, and blue.

The painter scoops a small amount of colored sand and lets it trickle between his fingers. He must be very skillful to make a straight line with sand. If he makes a mistake, he erases by covering the spot with more sand, and starts over again.

At the end of a day of ceremonies, the sandpainting is always destroyed and the sand scattered.

In Indian sandpainting and other forms of symbolized Indian art "The Great Mystery" of the universe is made an intimate part of daily life as follows:

"THE GREAT MYSTERY"

Sun: Our Father	**Morning Star:** Our Sister
Earth: Our Mother	**Milky Way:** Pathway of ghosts
Evening Star: Our Brother	**Northern Lights:** Campfires of our departed fathers

A large scrap book is a "must" for anyone wishing to start and develop an Indian lore hobby.

Your collection could include Indian pictures, designs, symbols, handcraft patterns, stories, your own art work, camp pictures, etc.

Materials You Can Use: Make the front and back covers out of heavy cardboard, plywood, plastic, and raw hide, or you can buy a large scrap book. You can cover the front and back with soft leather, chamois, wood-grained wall paper, oil cloth, felt, bright colored cloth, or aluminum foil.

How to Decorate Your Scrapbook: Here is an opportunity to stretch your imagination! A glance at Figs. 27 and 28 will give you an idea of how to make and decorate your scrap book.

Your scrap book can be covered with colored paper or wood-grained wall paper, with colored paper cut-out letters.

You can make a plywood cover, using a wood-burning set to inscribe the design.

A felt cover and colored felt appliqued letters and pictures makes an interesting book cover.

You can construct a heavy cardboard book with oil cloth, bright colored cloth, or soft leather covering.

You can consider a plywood cover, with cut-out letters of tin, aluminum, brass, copper, or colored plastic. Use small metal hinges.

A book cover and back can be made with plastic material. Lace it together with a leather thong.

A unique book cover can be designed with colored sand symbols. Make a stencil for your designs, then fill in with glue. Sprinkle colored sand on the fresh glue and let dry.

Front page designs and lettering can be made with match sticks, lollipop sticks, or small twigs glued on or tacked with small brads.

1/8" PLYWOOD COVER
WITH DESIGN
BURNED IN WITH
ELECTRIC NEEDLE

The
AMERICAN
INDIAN

(27)

HEAVY CARDBOARD
COVER WITH DIFFERENT
COLORED FELT PASTED
IN AREAS FIRST
SKETCHED IN.

LETTERS OF SMALL
TWIGS APPLIED WITH
MODEL CEMENT

(28)

INDIAN
CLUB

7. CEREMONIAL AND COUNCIL RING EQUIPMENT

PEACE PIPE INCANTATION TO THE FOUR WINDS

Oh ye of the East, be with us,
Oh ye of the dawn and day

Oh ye of the West, be with us,
Oh ye of the storm and nite

Oh ye of the South, behold us,
Oh ye of the path of the sun

Oh ye of the North, behold us,
Ye of the Mother of Day

INDIAN PIPES

THERE is little doubt that the tobacco pipe is of American origin. There is no mention of smoking in the Bible and we must begin our study of the custom near the end of the fifteenth century, the discovery of America, for information regarding our first knowledge of smoking the pipe.

Some pipes were very small, and some weighing several pounds were used only on special occasions such as treaty signings.

In North America, pipes varied according to locality; some were of a single piece, others had detachable stems.

The early cloud-blower of the Pueblos, a straight, tubular pipe, was used solely for ceremonial purposes. One end was simply enlarged to hold the tobacco, the stem being inserted in the opposite end. It had to be smoked by throwing back the head, which had a tendency to cause the tobacco to be drawn into the mouth; to prevent this, in some localities, a small pellet of clay was often inserted in the bowl.

Some ceremonial pipes were guarded by a specially appointed tribesman. The pipes were wrapped in fur or kept in a medicine bag, and sometimes stored in a special tent.

Some early pipes were made from the legbone of a deer or other animal, and quite often reinforced with a strip of rawhide, which, wrapped on wet, contracted in drying, helping to prevent the bone from splitting.

Some bowls would hold a thimbleful of tobacco and some an ounce or less.

The Iroquois pipe bowls were elaborately ornamented with figures of birds and animals. The Mound and Atlantic States Indians had the most artistically finished pipes, having a flat base with a highly polished bowl.

The bowl of the Sioux pipe is at a straight angle to the stem, and has a solid projection extending in front of the bowl.

The Chippewas used a smooth black stone, found in Central Wisconsin, and a red stone near Lake Superior. They were elaborately designed, highly polished and decorated with strips of beaver hide.

From Labrador to the Rocky Mountains the pipes had a bowl shaped like an acorn resting on a keel-like base.

The tomahawk pipe is made of metal with a bowl shaped like

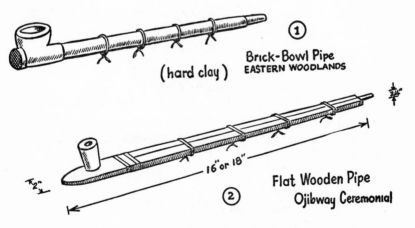

(hard clay)

① Brick-Bowl Pipe
EASTERN WOODLANDS

16" or 18"

② Flat Wooden Pipe
Ojibway Ceremonial

an acorn. Authorities do not know what tribes first made use of the tomahawk pipe, but believe that the crescent form is of Spanish design and the hatchet was English.

The Eastern Woodland Indians used short pipes with small stone or pottery bowls and wooden stems.

Indians of the Southern States used small pipes with bowls of pottery, stone, or wood with stems of wood or cane. The Cherokees made the best stone pipes with fine carvings of animals. The best pottery pipes were made by the Catawbas.

The Plains Indians used pipes with L-shaped or T-shaped bowls of red or black stone with wooden stems between twelve to fourteen inches long. They sometimes combined the pipe and war club and used pipe bags.

Indian Materials You Can Use for Bowl: Clay, wood, bone, claystone, soapstone, terra cotta, red and black stone, or pipestone (Catlinite).

Substitute Materials for Bowl: Plaster of Paris or balsa wood (non-smokable).

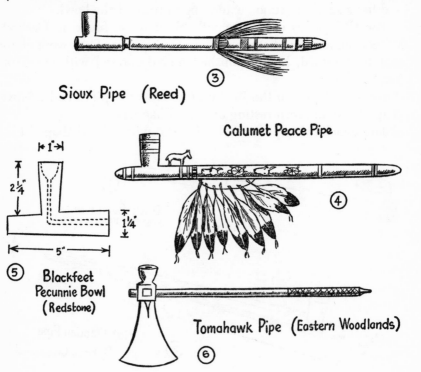

Sioux Pipe (Reed) ③

Calumet Peace Pipe ④

⑤ Blackfeet Pecunnie Bowl (Redstone)

Tomahawk Pipe (Eastern Woodlands) ⑥

Indian Materials You Can Use for Stem: Reed, cane, elder, sumac, bamboo, claystone, red or black softstone, any suitable splittable wood, or soft wood for flat type: black or white ash or witch hazel.

Substitute Materials for Stem: Balsa wood for reed or flat type (non-smokable).

Tools and Equipment You Will Need: Sharp knife, orange stick for modeling clay bowl, coping saw or hacksaw or light bandsaw, stiff, straight wire for burning the stem if desired, a wood burning outfit for designs, fine-toothed file, drill, and one-half inch bit.

Indian Decorations: Fur, hair, beads, quills, feathers, Indian dyes, thin strips of thong.

Substitute Decorations: Lacquers, oil paints, ribbons, airplane dope.

Instructions for Making Indian Pipe: If you decide to make a flat type pipe stem, as shown in Fig. 2, secure a piece of black or white ash or witch hazel, 16 or 18 inches long, 2 inches wide, and three quarters of an inch thick.

Plane and sand the top and bottom sides to a smooth finish.

Ream the channel with a stiff hot wire, working from both ends.

You can make a round pipe stem out of a hollow reed, bamboo, ash, sumac, elder, or any available, splittable wood. Split the stem, remove the pith or carve a channel and glue it together again. Lash it together with narrow strips of leather thong, as shown in Fig. 1, making sure to wet the thong before tying it around the stem.

Carve or model your pipe bowl out of wood, pipe-stone, soapstone, or clay. Drill hole with ½ inch bit. If you are fortunate enough in securing a piece of pipe-stone, (found in the southwest pipe-stone quarries or in trading posts), cut it to size with a hack saw, then carefully shape it with a fine-toothed file. See Fig. 5.

Imitation Balsa Wood Pipe: A good imitation, non-smokable ceremonial pipe can be made out of balsa wood, which can be bought in any hobby shop. You can make a flat type or round stem. The bowl is very easily carved out of balsa wood. It can be strengthened with an under-coating of airplane dope.

Instructions for Decorating Your Pipe: You can make a wooden bowl look like a pipe-stone bowl by buying a little red paint powder in any paint store and mixing it with a little water.

Paint your stem with bright colored oil paints or lacquer. Decorate it with feathers, as shown in Fig. 4. You can add horse hair, as shown in Fig. 3, and you can carve Indian figures, as shown in Fig. 4, or you can use a wood-burning set.

The illustrations below and on the following page show you an assortment of peace pipe bags and medicine pouches. The pouches, worn at Medicine Dances, Fig. 9, were made of animal skins and ornamented with porcupine or bird quills; and later beads were used. They were filled with bits of things which the Indians thought would please the good spirits and drive away the

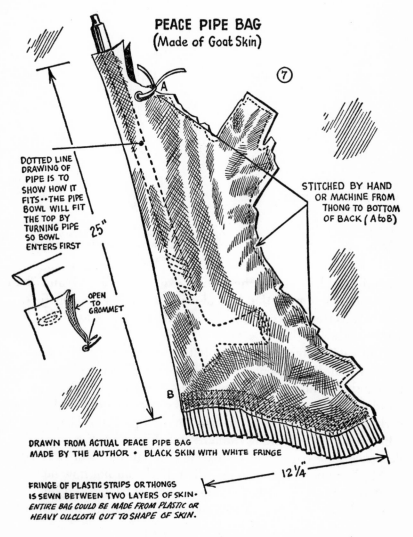

PEACE PIPE BAG
(Made of Goat Skin)

⑦

DOTTED LINE DRAWING OF PIPE IS TO SHOW HOW IT FITS··THE PIPE BOWL WILL FIT THE TOP BY TURNING PIPE SO BOWL ENTERS FIRST

25"

OPEN TO GROMMET

A

STITCHED BY HAND OR MACHINE FROM THONG TO BOTTOM OF BACK (A to B)

B

DRAWN FROM ACTUAL PEACE PIPE BAG MADE BY THE AUTHOR • BLACK SKIN WITH WHITE FRINGE

12 ¼"

FRINGE OF PLASTIC STRIPS OR THONGS IS SEWN BETWEEN TWO LAYERS OF SKIN· ENTIRE BAG COULD BE MADE FROM PLASTIC OR HEAVY OILCLOTH CUT TO SHAPE OF SKIN.

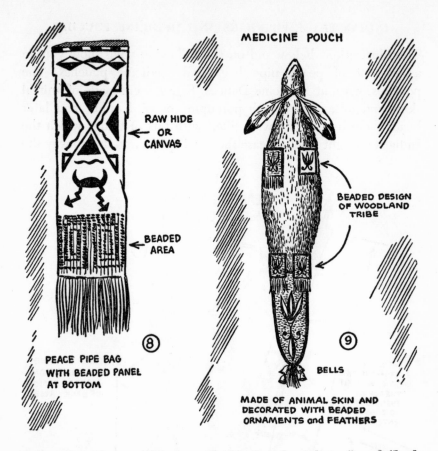

MEDICINE POUCH

RAW HIDE
← OR
CANVAS

BEADED DESIGN
OF WOODLAND
TRIBE

BEADED
AREA

⑧

PEACE PIPE BAG
WITH BEADED PANEL
AT BOTTOM

⑨

BELLS

MADE OF ANIMAL SKIN AND
DECORATED WITH BEADED
ORNAMENTS and FEATHERS

bad spirits. They called these things "good medicine" and "bad medicine." They used the skins of small animals sewn together.

Indian Materials You Can Use: Small animal skins and pieces of soft leather.

Substitute Materials: Canvas, felt, heavy cloth, and oil cloth.

Tools and Equipment You Will Need: Sharp knife, scissors, leather thong, large needle and strong thread.

Indian Decorations: Strips of bright colored cloth or felt, beadwork, soft leather strips for fringe work, oil paints or lacquer.

Instructions for Making Indian Peace Pipe Bag: Fig. 7 is a simple peace pipe bag made by a young Indian boy who was visiting Mt. Rushmore, and who proudly told the author how he made it out of a piece of goat skin about two feet long and one foot wide at the bottom. Simply fold the skin and sew the uneven side, leaving enough space at the top for the pipe to fit in the bag. Your shoemaker can sew it in a few minutes, or you can use a heavy black thread. Secure the top of the bag by punching two holes and tying it with a piece of leather thong. A black skin bag can be made even more striking looking by adding a fringe of white, soft leather fringe to the side and bottom.

Fig. 8 illustrates another type of peace pipe bag.

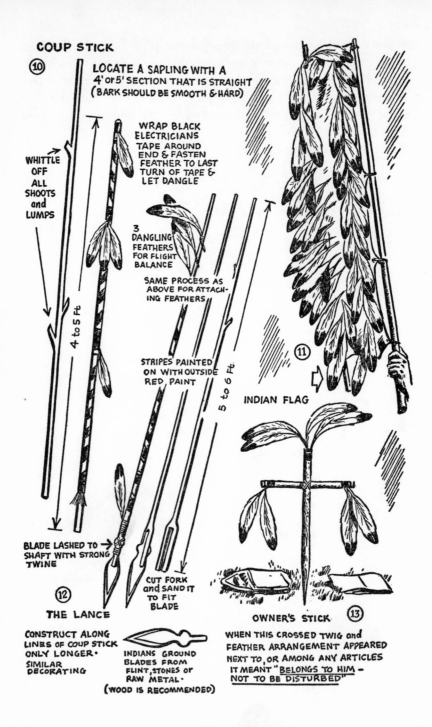

COUP STICK

(10) LOCATE A SAPLING WITH A 4' or 5' SECTION THAT IS STRAIGHT (BARK SHOULD BE SMOOTH & HARD)

WRAP BLACK ELECTRICIANS TAPE AROUND END & FASTEN FEATHER TO LAST TURN OF TAPE & LET DANGLE

WHITTLE OFF ALL SHOOTS and LUMPS

3 DANGLING FEATHERS FOR FLIGHT BALANCE

SAME PROCESS AS ABOVE FOR ATTACH-ING FEATHERS

4 to 5 ft.

STRIPES PAINTED ON WITH OUTSIDE RED PAINT

5 to 6 ft.

(11)

INDIAN FLAG

BLADE LASHED TO SHAFT WITH STRONG TWINE

CUT FORK and SAND IT TO FIT BLADE

(12)

THE LANCE

CONSTRUCT ALONG LINES OF COUP STICK ONLY LONGER. SIMILAR DECORATING

INDIANS GROUND BLADES FROM FLINT, STONES or RAW METAL. (WOOD IS RECOMMENDED)

OWNER'S STICK (13)

WHEN THIS CROSSED TWIG and FEATHER ARRANGEMENT APPEARED NEXT TO, OR AMONG ANY ARTICLES IT MEANT "BELONGS TO HIM - NOT TO BE DISTURBED"

The Indian Coup (coo) stick was the proud possession of the warrior. It was a long, slender, highly decorated staff, used by the Indian for counting "coup" in battle, which means striking or touching an enemy. The highest honor went to the Indian who did not kill his enemy, but merely touched a living enemy with his hand or coup stick.

How to Make a Coup Stick: Fig. 10 shows you how to pick a straight green sapling. It should reach from the ground to the tip of your fingers as you raise your arm above your head. Whittle off all bumps and knots and sand it to a smooth finish.

Decorate your coup stick with bright colored paints or carve Indian designs with a pen knife; tape it with strips of bright colored felt or tape; add feathers, horse hair, bits of fur, metal, and fluff feathers.

Fig. 11 is what the white man would call an Indian flag or standard. It was used for ceremonials, dances, and for war parties.

How to Make an Indian Flag: Secure a four or five foot sapling and prepare it in the same manner as described for making the coup stick. The feathers can be strung together from the top of the stick to the handle with heavy thread, piercing the quills in the same manner as described for threading the feathers on a war bonnet in Chapter 2.

HOW TO MAKE AN INDIAN LANCE

The Indian Lance, Fig. 12, can be made and decorated the same as the Coup Stick, adding feathers to the butt end for flight balance. Carve a fork to hold the blade, which can be made from wood. Lash the blade in the fork with leather thongs.

How to Make an Indian Owner's Stick: Fig. 13 is an Owner's Stick which was used by the Indian to mark his possessions, especially when leaving them unguarded while out of camp. It indicated to any passerby that the goods belonged to him and should not be disturbed. It usually consisted of two crossed twigs lashed with a leather thong and sometimes elaborately decorated with feathers, bits of fur, and bright colored paints or carvings.

A very important part of the warrior's outfit was the shield, with which he stopped or turned aside the arrows of his enemy. It was usually circular in shape, and was made of the tough hide of a buffalo's neck. It was even heavy enough to turn the ball of an old-fashioned smooth-bored gun. The shield was usually highly ornamented, and often had the warrior's "medicine" or lucky symbol painted on it, and was often fringed with eagle feathers.

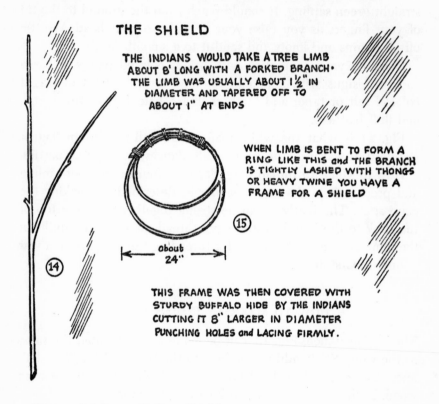

THE SHIELD

THE INDIANS WOULD TAKE A TREE LIMB ABOUT 8' LONG WITH A FORKED BRANCH. THE LIMB WAS USUALLY ABOUT 1½" IN DIAMETER AND TAPERED OFF TO ABOUT 1" AT ENDS

WHEN LIMB IS BENT TO FORM A RING LIKE THIS and THE BRANCH IS TIGHTLY LASHED WITH THONGS OR HEAVY TWINE YOU HAVE A FRAME FOR A SHIELD

(15)

about 24"

(14)

THIS FRAME WAS THEN COVERED WITH STURDY BUFFALO HIDE BY THE INDIANS CUTTING IT 8" LARGER IN DIAMETER PUNCHING HOLES and LACING FIRMLY.

How to Make an Indian Shield.

Indian Materials You Can Use: Raw hide or sheepskin, leather thong for lacing, pliable tree limb with one forked branch.

Substitute Materials: Make a shield out of plywood or a peach basket cover. Use a wooden or metal barrel hoop for the frame, which could be covered with oil cloth, burlap, canvas, bright colored cloth, or plastic.

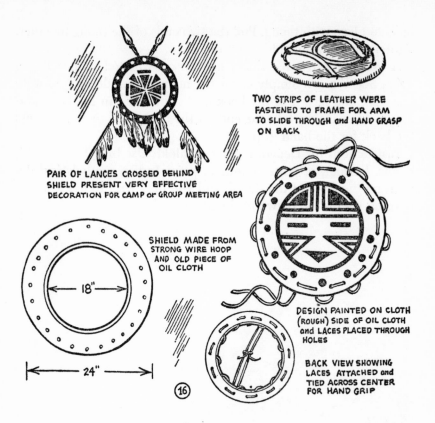

PAIR OF LANCES CROSSED BEHIND SHIELD PRESENT VERY EFFECTIVE DECORATION FOR CAMP or GROUP MEETING AREA

TWO STRIPS OF LEATHER WERE FASTENED TO FRAME FOR ARM TO SLIDE THROUGH and HAND GRASP ON BACK

SHIELD MADE FROM STRONG WIRE HOOP AND OLD PIECE OF OIL CLOTH

DESIGN PAINTED ON CLOTH (ROUGH) SIDE OF OIL CLOTH and LACES PLACED THROUGH HOLES

BACK VIEW SHOWING LACES ATTACHED and TIED ACROSS CENTER FOR HAND GRIP

Tools and Equipment You Will Need: Scissors for cutting material or shears for cutting leather, leather thong for lacing, awl, and paint brush.

Indian Decorations: Indian dyes or paints, feathers, horse hair and animal tails, beads.

Substitute Decorations: Oil paints, water or poster paints, lacquers or crayons. Wood burning set can be used to design the plywood shield, feathers, bits of bright colored cloth or ribbon.

Instructions for Making Shield: Carefully pick out a green, pliable tree limb about one inch in diameter, with one forked branch, as illustrated in Fig. 14. Bend the limbs to form a circle and tightly lash together with heavy cord or thin leather thong, as shown in Fig. 15. Now cover the frame with the hide, which should be about 8 inches larger than the diameter of the frame. Punch holes about two inches apart around the inside edge of the hide and lace with thong. Pull the two ends of the thong together, tightening the whole hide, and tie off.

A very easy-to-make shield can be constructed with a barrel hoop. See Fig. 16. Simply cover the hoop with hide or substitute material, and lace it in the back as just outlined in the last paragraph. After lacing, take the ends of the thong and tie them across the back for the hand grip.

Instructions for Decorating Your Shield: Use bright colored oil paints, lacquer, or poster paints to paint Indian symbols and designs on the front of the shield, and you may wish to use a woodburning set on the plywood shield.

KACHINA DOLLS
(*Sometimes spelled Katchinas*)

The Hopi Indians of Arizona perform a Kachina ceremony every year from about December 21st until July. The costumed dancers wear masks, impersonating supernatural spirits, called Kachinas. The Indians believed that they brought them the good things of life.

Some of these dances are performed in the village kivas (kee-wahs) and not open to the public, and some of them are staged in the village plaza for everyone to see.

The Kachina dancers bring gifts for the children in the manner of the white man's Santa Claus.

Before the yearly Kachina ceremonies, the Indian artists carve small wooden figures (Tehu or Kachina dolls) representing the various Kachinas which are to be presented to the children.

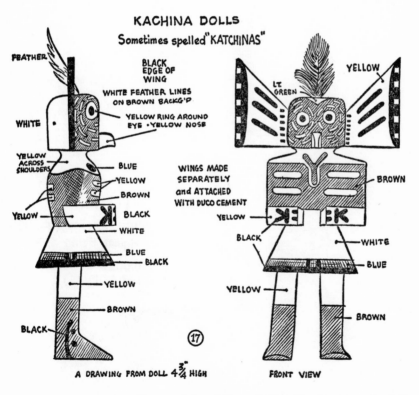

KACHINA DOLLS

Sometimes spelled "KATCHINAS"

FEATHER
BLACK EDGE OF WING
WHITE FEATHER LINES ON BROWN BACKG'D
YELLOW RING AROUND EYE • YELLOW NOSE
WHITE
YELLOW ACROSS SHOULDERS
BLUE
YELLOW
BROWN
YELLOW
BLACK
WHITE
BLUE
BLACK
YELLOW
BROWN
BLACK

WINGS MADE SEPARATELY and ATTACHED WITH DUCO CEMENT

YELLOW
LT GREEN
YELLOW
BROWN
YELLOW
BLACK
WHITE
BLUE
YELLOW
BROWN

⑰

A DRAWING FROM DOLL 4¾" HIGH

FRONT VIEW

Ceremonial and Council Ring Equipment / 149

They are made from the roots of the cottonwood tree. The village artists carve them with a knife and smooth them down. The ears, noses and beaks are cut out separately and glued on. Then they are painted with bright colors, using very little water.

Figs. 17 and 18 illustrate two small Kachina dolls. Fig. 17 is the author's favorite Kachina, made by Manual Suage, the Medicine Man of Taos, New Mexico. Fig. 18 is a simpler design. Use cottonwood roots if available. If not, any soft wood will do. You can substitute balsa wood for fast and easy cutting.

An excellent set of heavy cardboard "cut and color" Kachina dolls is published by the Eukabi Publishers, Old Albuquerque, New Mexico.

BIBLIOGRAPHY: *Kachinas and Kachina Dolls*, Leaflet No. 111, Denver Art Museum, Denver, Colorado.

Kachina Dolls, The Hopi Indians, Harry C. James, Caxton Printers, Ltd., Caldwell, Idaho.

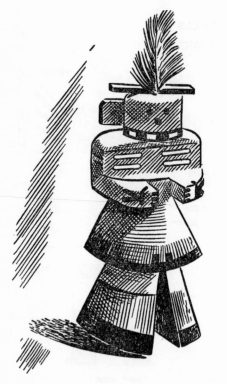

ANOTHER KACHINA FIGURE
The Original Being 4" Tall

(DECORATED IN SAME COLOR SCHEME)

⑱

Fig. 19 is an Indian doll with a corncob center. It would make an excellent present for a boy to present to his little sister.

Make an Indian dress out of a piece of chamois, fitting it about an inch below the largest end of the corn cob. Add eyes, nose, and mouth with poster paint, and sew some dark corn silk on top for hair.

The hands can be made out of a tiny bit of corn husk or cob. Paper feet can be pinned to the bottom of the cob.

Decorate the dress with beadwork or painted designs.

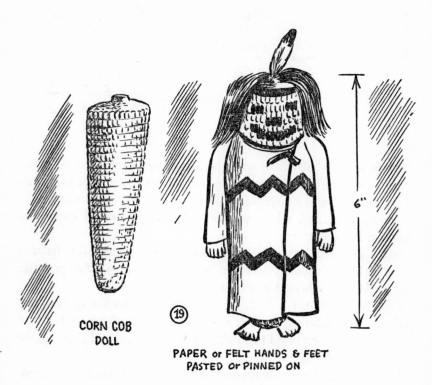

CORN COB
DOLL

⑲

PAPER or FELT HANDS & FEET
PASTED or PINNED ON

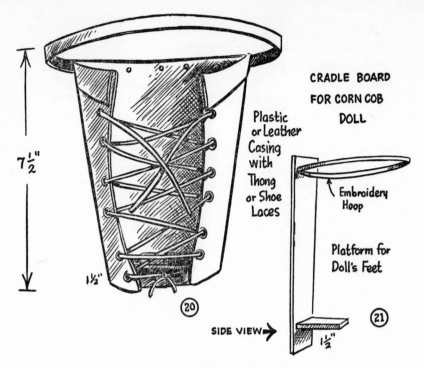

CRADLE BOARD
FOR CORN COB
DOLL

Plastic
or Leather
Casing
with
Thong
or Shoe
Laces

7½"

1½"

Embroidery
Hoop

Platform for
Doll's Feet

20

21

SIDE VIEW➡

1½"

INDIAN CRADLE BOARD

Most of Indian babyhood was spent tied to a cradle board in security and comfort. He was taken out of his wrappings each day to be cleaned and massaged. The baby was always within sight of its mother, and when walking about, she would carry the child on her back.

Some authorities say that the cradle board gave the baby a great feeling of security and also helped to develop a fine posture. The child was released when he was ready to walk.

Fig. 20 illustrates a Plains cradle board, which any boy can make for his sister's doll. It is a simple wood backing with a foot step and a wooden band to shade the baby's eyes, and also a place to hang some beads.

Fig. 21 is a miniature cradle board for the corn cob or commercial Indian doll. It is a simple piece of thin wood (cigar box top will do nicely for a small doll) with a small foot rest glued or tacked to the board. The canopy can be an embroidery hoop, tacked or glued to the top of the board.

Indians enjoy wearing masks during dances and ceremonials just as white men like to wear them on Halloween and to masquerade parties. The early Indians used animal heads to stalk game. In addition to wearing masks for fun, they wore them for religious reasons, serious ceremonials and dances.

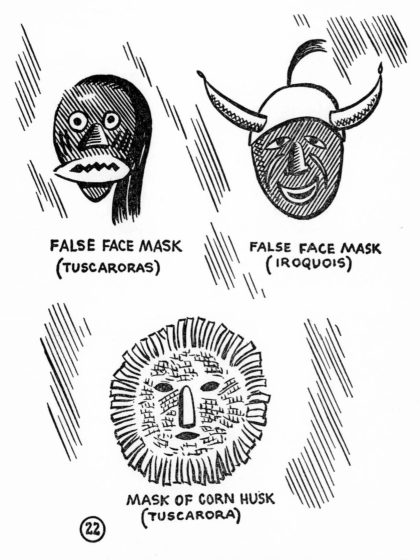

FALSE FACE MASK
(TUSCARORAS)

FALSE FACE MASK
(IROQUOIS)

MASK OF CORN HUSK
(TUSCARORA)

22

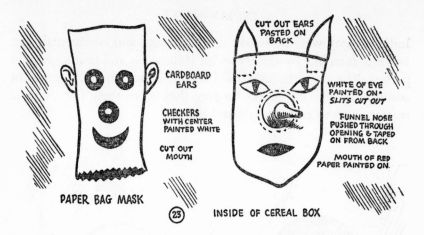

PAPER BAG MASK

(23) INSIDE OF CEREAL BOX

CUT OUT EARS PASTED ON BACK

CARDBOARD EARS

CHECKERS WITH CENTER PAINTED WHITE

CUT OUT MOUTH

WHITE OF EYE PAINTED ON. SLITS CUT OUT

FUNNEL NOSE PUSHED THROUGH OPENING & TAPED ON FROM BACK

MOUTH OF RED PAPER PAINTED ON.

They made them out of many materials including wood, bone, cloth, bark, and leather. They added all kinds of gay decorations such as bits of metal, beads, horse hair and large wooden framed fans on top, and they painted them with bright colored paints in fantastic geometrical, human and animal designs (Fig. 22).

Fig. 23 shows you how to make masks out of heavy paper bags, and cereal boxes. You can also use the crown of an old hat and colored heavy paper. Add cardboard ears, nose, and beak. Stick feathers in the top and sides. Sew colored yarn on for hair. Color them with crayons or bright colored oil paints or poster paints. Make them as fantastic as you like.

BIBLIOGRAPHY: *Types of Indian Masks,* Leaflet 65-66, Denver Art Museum, Denver, Colorado. This is one of the best, most concise references describing 32 Indian masks.

Masks–A. C. Fletcher, *Bulletin 30,* Part 2, 1907, Bureau of American Ethnology.

Randolph Plastics–Churchtown-Hollowville Rd., R.D. 2, Hudson, N. Y. Commercial plastic reproductions of ceremonial masks used in the Long House, hence not considered "tabu" in accordance with Indian tradition. High quality and authentic detail.

8. FIRE BUILDING

W HITE man makes big fire and runs away. Indian makes small fire and sits close." There are four kinds of campfires: the "warming up" fire, the "cooking" fire, the "smudge" fire to drive away mosquitoes, and the "friendship" fire, where you sit around and talk or just silently watch the flames.

① THE TIPI

② THE LOG CABIN

Fig. 1 is a single "tipi" campfire. It can be made small enough to serve a few, or it can be made with split logs for a large camp or council fire.

Fig. 2 is the "log cabin" campfire, which can be made for a small group (short sticks of wood) or for a large camp or council fire, using logs, graduating to limbs and sticks, as you near the top of the campfire. Be sure to fill the center with small twigs, brush, and dry grass.

Select a sheltered and safe place to build your cooking fire, where no wind can blow it out or into the surrounding dry brush.

Next in importance is the wood. Certain kinds of wood, such as hickory, oak, birch, beech, hard maple, ash, elm, locust, long-leaf pine, and cherry, have fairly high heat values. Laboratory tests show that one cord of seasoned wood of these species is equal to one ton of good coal. Comparatively low heat woods include short leaf maple, hemlock, sycamore, cedar, poplar, Norway pine, cypress, basswood, spruce, and white pine, although they ignite readily and give out a quick hot flame, but one that soon dies down. Resinous pines give off an oily black smoke.

Woods good for back logs are: green red oak, green elm, green maple, and green poplars.

The woodsmen of British Columbia have a wood-chopping trick that keeps nicks out of the axe blade. When chopping the wood, instead of laying it on a block or on the ground where you have a chance to miss and put a nick in your axe, just stand it on end, holding it with the left hand at a convenient angle and strike glancing blows into it, turning the limb till you have gone all the way round, as shown in Fig. 3. It will then break with a blow from the head of the axe, and you have a nice feathery end to catch fire easily.

A "fire-lighter" or "fuzz-stick" can be made by taking a dry, resinous stick, about an inch thick, and shaving it with a good sharp jackknife into thin slivers, which remain on the stick. See Fig. 4. Three or four "fuzz-sticks" will insure the starting of a fire.

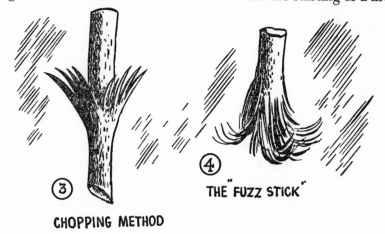

③ CHOPPING METHOD

④ THE "FUZZ STICK"

There are three ways of building a fire without matches. The simplest, but very difficult, is the rubbing together of two sticks or hand drills; the second, by use of a bow drill; and third, by the use of flint and steel.

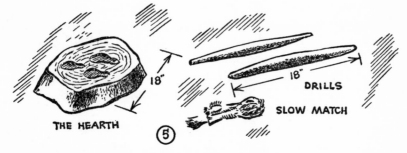

THE HEARTH · ⑤ · 18" · 18" · DRILLS · SLOW MATCH

Fig. 5 is a good illustration of the simplest sort of fire drill, one used by the Indians of Washington and the Northwest. Following is a description of the set, quoted by special permission from the Smithsonian Report, "Firemaking Apparatus in the United States National Museum," by Dr. Walter Hough:

"It consists of a hearth, two drills, and a slow match. The hearth is a rounded piece of cedar wood; opposite the fire-holes it is dressed flat, so as to rest firmly on the ground. There are three fire-holes with wide notches. The drills taper to each end; that is, are larger in the middle. The powder, a fine brown dust, collects at the junction of the slot and fire-hole, where they form a lip, and there readily ignites. This side of the hearth is semi-decayed. No doubt the slots were cut in that side for the purpose of utilizing this quality. The drills are bulged toward the middle, thereby rendering it possible to give great pressure and at the same time rapid rotation without allowing the hands to slip down too rapidly, a fault in many fire drills. The slow match is of frayed cedar bark, about a yard long, folded squarely together, and used section by section." Mr. Willoughby says:

"The stick with three cavities was placed upon the ground, the Indian kneeling and placing a knee upon each end. He placed one end of the smaller stick in one of the cavities, and, holding the other end between the palms of his hands, kept up a rapid, half-rotary motion, causing an amount of friction sufficient to produce fire. With this he lighted the end of the braided slow-match of cedar bark. This was often carried for weeks thus ignited and held carefully beneath the blanket to protect it from wind and rain.

"Fire is easily produced with this set. It takes but a slight effort to cause a wreath of aromatic smoke to curl up, and the friction easily grinds off a dark powder, which collects between the edges of the slot.

"When this ignites, it drops down the slot in little pellets, and falls upon the tinder placed below to receive it. Both drill and hearth are eighteen inches long."

Making fire by friction with a bow drill is the most common method used by Indians from Alaska to South America. See Fig. 6. Twist the Bow Cord, (B) once around the Drill, (C). Place the point of the Drill into the hole on the Block (D). Place the hand Block (A) on the top of the Drill and draw back and forth on the bow creating a friction that will eventually develop a volume of smoke. Now fan the smoking powder and place the Tinder (E), a wad of dry grass, fine strands of cedar or birch bark on the spark and blow on it till it bursts into flame.

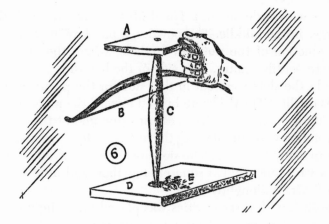

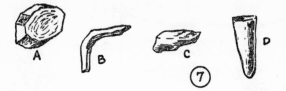

The third method of building a fire is with a flint and steel, adopted by the Indians from the white man, and now in use by some remote tribes. See Fig. 7. It consists of a select piece of absolutely dry punk wood (A), a piece of hard steel with a sharp striking surface (B), a selected piece of flint (C) which may take some experimenting to find just the right piece, and a tinder horn (D), made from the tip end of a cow's horn. Simply place the dry tinder in the horn, direct the sparks into it, and when a tiny bit of smoke rises, blow carefully into a flame and place the burning tinder on the fuzz-sticks and previously arranged dry twigs.

INDIAN COOKING FIRES AND METHODS

A wide variety of Indian cooking fires are illustrated on the following pages.

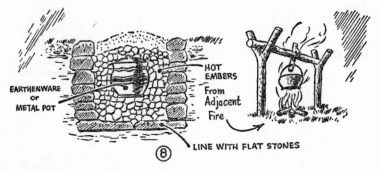

Fig. 8 is an Indian underground oven pit. The construction is fully described in Chapter 9, Indian Foods and Cooking.

Fig. 9 clearly outlines the making of a food cooler with canvas on the dirt floor, the walls of flat stones. The removable covering is made by lashing poles together, then covering with straw, brush, and tall grass.

Fig. 10 is a simple Sleep Fire, which can also be used as a cooking fire. Be sure to pick very dry wood for this fire.

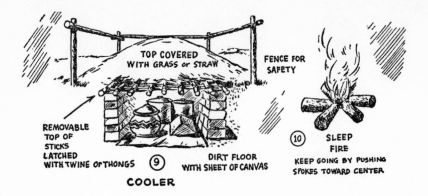

TOP COVERED
WITH GRASS or STRAW

FENCE FOR
SAFETY

REMOVABLE
TOP OF
STICKS
LATCHED
WITH TWINE or THONGS ⑨

DIRT FLOOR
WITH SHEET OF CANVAS

COOLER

⑩ SLEEP
FIRE
KEEP GOING BY PUSHING
SPOKES TOWARD CENTER

Fig. 11 is an Indian Roasting Fire, with green logs for the reflector. The "spit" that holds the piece of meat can be a green limb with a notched end for turning the meat.

Fig. 12 is a large, flat stone cooking fire built on top of stones.

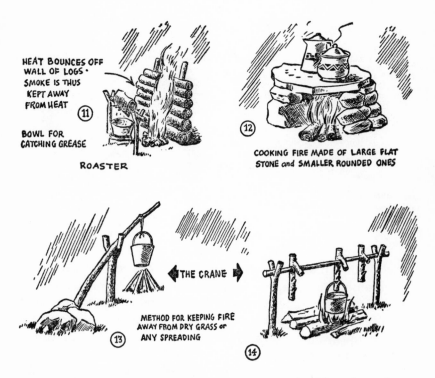

HEAT BOUNCES OFF
WALL OF LOGS ·
SMOKE IS THUS
KEPT AWAY
FROM HEAT
⑪

BOWL FOR
CATCHING GREASE

ROASTER

⑫

COOKING FIRE MADE OF LARGE FLAT
STONE and SMALLER ROUNDED ONES

⬅ THE CRANE ➡

METHOD FOR KEEPING FIRE
AWAY FROM DRY GRASS or
⑬ ANY SPREADING

⑭

Fig. 13 and 14 show you two more ways to build cooking fires.

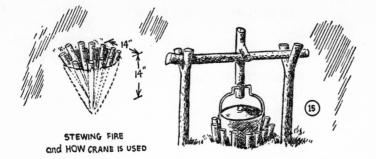

STEWING FIRE
and HOW CRANE IS USED

Fig. 15 shows you how to make a stewing fire, which is especially good for a windy day.

Fig. 16 shows you how to eliminate a lot of back aches for the camp cook by raising the cooking surface of the fire.

Fig. 17 is a fast burning criss cross or log cabin cooking fire. Don't forget to make enough fuzz sticks for a quick start.

METHOD FOR RAISING FIRE
OFF GROUND WITH FLAT STONES

FUZZ STICK

FAST BURNING CRISS-CROSS or
LOG CABIN COOKING FIRE

CARE WITH CAMP FIRES

Never build a camp fire against a tree or log, in leaf mold or in rotten wood. Build all fires away from overhanging branches and on a dirt or rock foundation. Dig all rotten wood or leaf mold from the fire pit and scrape away all inflammable material within a radius of from three to five feet. Make sure that the fire cannot spread on or under the ground or up the moss or bark of a tree while you are in camp, and that it is going to be easy to extinguish when you are ready to leave.

Figs. 18 and 19 are two simple but very handy roasting, broiling, and frying gadgets. Be sure to make them with green limbs.

Fig. 20 is a notch stick for holding pots over the fire.

Fig. 21 is a baked potato lifter, made with 2 green sticks. One stick has a 'Y' end, and the other one is straight.

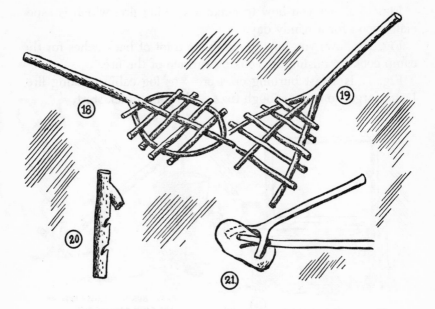

WHEN YOU QUIT CAMP

Never leave a camp fire, even for a short time, without completely extinguishing every spark with water or fresh dirt free from moss or leaf mold. Do not throw charred cross logs to one side where a smouldering spark might catch. It is well to soak thoroughly all embers and charred pieces of wood and then cover them with dirt. Feel around the outer edge of the fire pit to make sure no fire is smouldering in charred roots or leaf mold. (Fires escape each year after campers thought they were extinguished).

FIREHORN CARRIER

"When the Blackfeet traveled, they carried their fire along with them. A buffalo horn was lined with moist, rotten wood, and slung over the shoulder by a thong. The open end of the horn was fitted with a wooden stopper. With the signal to march, the carrier of the fire-horn took a live coal from the one remaining fire and put it in the fire-horn. He then carefully extinguished the last campfire. On top of the coal within his horn, the firebearer placed a piece of punk that came from a fungus growth found on birch trees.

"The horn was then tightly closed, and the punk smouldered within its airtight chamber. When needed, new punk was added. The first young men who reached the appointed camp ground gathered brush and wood and formed piles in three different places.

"As soon as the fire-horn carrier arrived, he hastened to one of the piles, turned out his glowing punk, and tended it until the fire was lighted. The other wood piles were kindled from this one.

"When the women arrived and the lodges were set up, they started their own cooking fires from the three that were lighted first."

—From *Indians of Yesterday*, Marion E. Gridley. Reprinted by permission, M. A. Donohue & Co., New York, N. Y.

9. FOODS AND COOKING

INDIAN FOODS

W E OWE the Indian almost everything, including our country. But most important of all, the whole world's most useful and essential foods have been received from the Indian. A few of the foods, unknown to the rest of the world before the coming of the white man to our shores, include: maize (corn), hominy, white potatoes, buckwheat, pumpkin, squashes, many kinds of melons and fruit, sunflower seeds, tomatoes, lima and string beans, berries, nuts, herbs, spices, peanuts, wild rice, peppers, onions, maple syrup, and the wild turkey. The tender leaves and buds of the milk-weed and the fronds of ferns were eaten as greens by the Indians. The roots and seeds of the yellow pond lily were a special treat. Maple syrup was often used as a substitute for salt. Water was the most common drink, although many drinks were made from berry juice.

Indians also drank tea made with sassafras roots, sweet birch twigs, wintergreen, and leaves of young strawberry plants.

Besides the foods that the Indian raised, there were many large game animals such as the deer, elk, bear, buffalo, and the moose; and small game such as squirrels, opossums, ground hogs; and also wild turkeys, quail, pheasants, and many kinds of fish.

Salt was obtained from the salt lakes.

Food and Cooking

AMONG THE NORTH AMERICAN INDIANS

CALIFORNIA FOODS
(*Seed Gatherers*)

The seed gatherers of California had very few animals to hunt and most of their meat came from rabbits; there were lakes where they found ducks, fish, and mud hens, but their chief food was nuts and seeds. The Pomo and Maidu in California practically lived on acorns. They pounded it into flour with a stone, washed out the bitter taste with water, and made it into thick soup cooked by hot stones dropped into a tightly-woven basket.

NORTHEASTERN FOODS

From the New England and southeastern states and westward to
Minnesota and south of the Ohio River, the Indians found large
game animals, including the deer, bear and moose, flocks of wild
pigeons, ducks, geese, wild turkeys, partridge, quail, pheasant,
and many water birds. The rivers and lakes were full of many
kinds of fish.

They also had corn, sunflower seeds, beans, squash, fruits,
berries, nuts, and tender leaves.

SOUTHWESTERN FOODS

Wild turkey was a favorite with the People of the Mesas, and
they also enjoyed deer meat. They depended much upon corn.
After the Spaniards came, they acquired sheep and became great
shepherds. They enjoyed the fruit of the saguaro cactus and the
pinon nut. Among some southwestern tribes such as the Apache,
Navaho, and Zuni, fish was taboo as food.

FOOD ON THE PLAINS

The Plains Indians enjoyed eating buffalo meat, fresh or dried,
and deer meat.

Pemmican was another favorite food, and this was made of
pounded dried meat, dried berries or fruit, and buffalo fat.

SOUTHEASTERN FOODS

The southeastern Indians cultivated beans, squashes, two varieties of sweet potatoes, pumpkins, and the sunflower, wild fruits,
roots, and berries.

NORTHWESTERN FOODS

The north coast Indian knew nothing of the buffalo and he did
not raise any crops. The rivers ran thick with salmon and within
the sea were halibut, seals, and whales. The people ate the flesh
of bear, deer, and moose, yet it was on the salmon that they de-

MAIDEN REMOVING HOT STONE FROM FIRE TO PLACE IT
IN FOOD BASKET • After the painting by Holmes

pended the year around. Wild berries and plenty of roots grew
in great quantities and these provided them with vegetable food.

A leader of the community, when giving a potlatch, would pro-
vide large quantities of the finest of foods, including fresh or
dried salmon. There would be cakes made of dried berries, tender
roots and seeds good to eat. There would be seal, whale, or bear
meat, and halibut. The food was dipped into dishes of warm grease
or fish oil for added flavor!

The Indians who lived close to the seacoast enjoyed clams,
oysters, and other shell fish, and the hard shells were used in
many ways; in fact, the Pilgrims enjoyed their first clam bake as
guests of the Indian. The early settlers thought they were poisonous, along with the tomatoes.

FOOD PRESERVATION

Foods were preserved by drying, and sometimes strung or tied in
bundles for easy transportation and storage. Animal foods were
often dried or frozen, and sometimes preserved by smoking. Dried
meat was sometimes pulverized and mixed with berries and
grease, making pemmican, which was carried in parfleches. Fruits

were pulped and dried for preservation. Sometimes nuts were ground before storing.

RANDOM . . .

The Indian cooked most of his food. Only in cases of extreme emergency would he eat raw food. . . . It was the early custom of many tribes to serve one meal a day, usually in the middle of the morning. This was particularly true of the early Iroquois, who lived in communal Long Houses. . . . Sugar was produced by evaporation of maple sap in New England. When the maple sap ran in the early spring the liquid was collected in kettles made of birch bark and hung over the fire until it thickened. It was then poured into molds of bark or wood and left to harden. Sometimes it was spread on the snow which hardened it like candy. . . . The process of cross-pollination seems to have been known to the early Indians. . . . Indians enjoyed popcorn. . . . Tobacco, too, was another agricultural gift of the Indian that became of great commercial worth. . . . Today, more than half of the varieties of vegetables grown in our gardens came from the Indian. . . . It was the Woodland Indians who played hosts for the first Thanksgiving feast. . . . The Iroquois name for maize (corn) means "our life". . . . Succotash is an Indian word for a mixture of corn and beans. . . . In Bulletin 30, Food, pg. 467, Bureau of American Ethnology, we are told that, in general, in the *northern portion* of the continent the diet was three-fourths animal food; in the *southern part* it was three-fourths vegetable; while in the tribes of the *coast, mountains, lakes,* and *plains* the diet varied according to the food supply. . . . The early Navaho Indian counted among the booty of war: "corn, gourds, and other field products". . . . The Papago Indians of Arizona harvest the sweet fruit of the saguaro cactus (sah-war-o). . . . The fruit is cleaned and boiled. After straining, the pulp is laid out to dry and the rest is made into jam. . . . The Chippewa Indians enjoyed wild rice.

INDIAN COOKING METHODS

Most Indian cooking was done by roasting, boiling, grilling, and baking. Vegetables were usually roasted in ashes or in pits over hot stones. Meat was usually boiled, sometimes broiled and roasted. Native clay pots were used for cooking, but the coming of the white man brought metal pots. Baking was done in adobe ovens or upon flat stones laid over a fire.

COOKING STONES

"In the Madison Museum in Yellowstone National Park on display in the middle case can be found a round stone called a 'cooking stone.' Stones such as this hold an important place in the methods of Indian food preparation.

"Not all cooking stones were of the same size, nor were they of similar shape. However, they were generally small, about the size of a man's fist, so that they could be handled easily with a pair of tongs made of a split log of proper length to keep the handler from being burned as he lifted the stones from the fire. These tongs were about 4 feet long and 2 inches in diameter. Fires were built in small depressions in the ground, the rocks were placed in the glowing embers, and were removed from the fire when the cook needed them during preparation of the food. They were then dropped into whatever containers held the food and the heat was sufficient for cooking."

From—*Yellowstone's Bannock Indian Trails* by Wayne F. Replogle, The Yellowstone Library & Museum Association, Yellowstone Park, Wyoming. Reprinted by permission.

CORN

Corn was prepared in a number of ways. A favorite method, employed today in many Boy Scout and YMCA camps, is to dig a deep hole in the ground in preparation for placing large stones in the bottom. Then a log fire is kept burning for a long time, sometimes over-night. After most of the ashes have been cleared away, the stones are covered with corn stalks and husks. Then the ears of corn are placed in the pit and covered with more corn stalks and husks. Water is poured over the top and covered with dirt. You can add a modern touch by covering everything with a heavy water-soaked tarpaulin before the earth is packed down.

Let the corn steam all day. The whole camp can participate in this ceremony. The same procedure can be used when filling large metal containers with beans.

Boiled cornbread was made by hulling, washing, and pounding the corn into flour. The flour was mixed with boiling water until it became a dough-like substance. Sometimes beans, nuts, and berries were added to the dough. It was then kneaded into loaves and placed in boiling water for about an hour. The bread was ready when it floated to the top.

Pumpkin or squash boiled with apples and maple sugar makes a delicious Indian pudding.

Corn Cakes—green corn scraped from the cob and baked. Mash the corn up, mold it into desired shapes, dust with fine cornmeal. Place cakes in a fresh corn husk and bake in hot ashes as roasting ears.

(See Chapter 8 for Indian Cooking Fires and Methods.)

SUGGESTED INDIAN MENUS

Quail or Turkey, sweet potatoes, succotash, tomatoes, wild honey, cornbread, strawberries, pumpkin pie, maple sugar candy, assorted nuts.

Venison, baked potatoes, squash, tomatoes, currant jelly, corn cakes, strawberries, baked apples, maple sugar candy, assorted nuts.

Steamed clams or fish, baked potatoes, squash, tomatoes, wild honey, cornbread, blackberries, watermelon, maple sugar candy, assorted nuts.

Stewed rabbit, sweet potatoes, corn on cob, tomatoes, currant jelly, corn cakes, blackberries, muskmelon, maple sugar candy, assorted nuts.

Beverage: Peppermint or sassafras tea, papaya juice. Maple sugar dissolved in cold water is pleasantly refreshing.

Additional regional and seasonal foods: Buffalo steak, cranberries, beach plum, Jerusalem artichoke, turtle soup, huckleberries, ripe persimmon,—and chestnut filling for the turkey!

HOW TO PLANT AN INDIAN GARDEN

While the subsistence of the people was largely derived from hunting and fishing, or from the wild fruits of the earth, yet a very large proportion of the tribes practised agriculture. This is especially true of those which inhabited the country of abundant rainfall lying between the Atlantic Ocean and the Mississippi River. Yet it was by no means confined to these alone, for many tribes of the high dry plains, of Pawnee, Dakota, and, in ancient times, Algonquin stock, raised crops of corn, beans, and squashes.

Indians used wooden diggers and hoes, and sometimes the shoulder of an animal for preparing the garden soil.

Make rows of small hills about two feet apart. Plant three or four corn kernels in each hill. A small piece of fish was added to the hill by the Indians for fertilizer.

You can also add a few beans in the hill and they will grow up the corn stalk, and use it for a bean pole. You can also scatter squash and pumpkin seeds; as they grow, they will twine in around the base of the small hills.

Indians said that corn, bean, and squash plants were three sisters and should always be planted together.

GOURDS

Growing gourds is becoming an increasingly popular hobby.

They are shapely, have majestic colors, strange markings, are so very unlike each other; they are decorative and simple to grow. You plant them and care for them the same as you would a cucumber, except they should be grown on a trellis off the ground.

The Indians grew gourds out of necessity. The dried and cured gourds served the Indian in many ways. The smaller ones were decorated or painted in bright colors and were used as rattles in their ceremonial dances. The largest ones were cut and formed into bowls which were used for food and also drinking cups.

The early Navaho Indians counted gourds among the booty of war.

Dried and cured gourds should be waxed or shellacked to bring out their natural color.

For those interested in cultivating gourd raising as a hobby, we suggest addressing a request for complete information to H. John Harder, Mgr., Joy Industries, 1547 S. Cloverdale, Los Angeles, 19, California.

10. IMPLEMENTS AND UTENSILS

STONE: (Figs. 1 and 2) The early Indian had no knowledge of metals, but he fashioned a stone hammer, an axe, and a very effective war club. Hammers and axes were usually made out of two kinds of stones. Granite was used for pounding tools, but the Indians had difficulty in making sharp axes. The Northwest Indians used an adze made of hard serpentine or jade. Corn was ground by rubbing small hand stones on large flat ones.

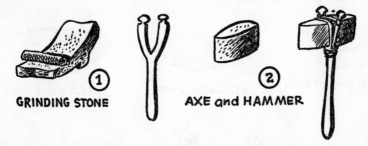

GRINDING STONE   ①   AXE and HAMMER   ②

A second kind of stone would split; such as flint, chert, and the black volcanic glass called obsidian. With these the Indians used a chipping process. The edge of a stone was placed on a piece of wood; the Indian would press a bone chisel against it and hammer until a chip would fly off. Knocking off a row of chips would create a cutting edge for a stone knife. The shorter pieces would become skin scrapers, spearheads, and arrowheads.

Stone pots and mortars were used by the Southwest and coast Indians.

Bone: (Fig. 3) Pieces of bone would be broken into sharp slivers and used for awls, eyeless needles, and chisels. Bone knives and scrapers were also made. Many of these tools were fitted into a forked stick and then bound with twisted fiber plant or animal sinew.

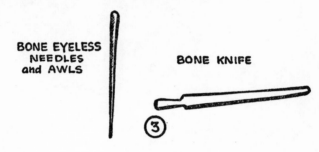

BONE EYELESS NEEDLES and AWLS

BONE KNIFE

Wood: (Figs. 4 and 5) Forked wooden sticks were used for planting. The Indian also used a wooden hoe shaped like a sword with a sharp edge. He pulled it along the ground to cut off the weeds.

Fungus and knots on trees were used for bowls and dishes. Stone pots and mortars were used by the southwest coast Indians.

Boxes, buckets, and dishes were made out of birch bark with tree gum used for binding.

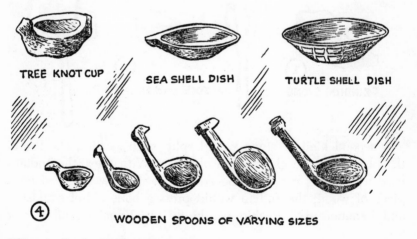

TREE KNOT CUP   SEA SHELL DISH   TURTLE SHELL DISH

WOODEN SPOONS OF VARYING SIZES

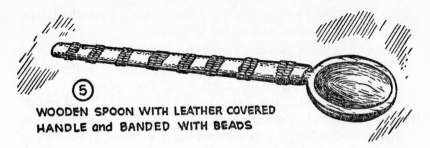

5

WOODEN SPOON WITH LEATHER COVERED
HANDLE and BANDED WITH BEADS

Some Plains Indians used mortars of hard wood with a long wooden pestle. Cups were made from the lining of animal entrails and some tribes wove baskets so tight that they could hold water and be used for cooking after the water had been heated with hot stones.

Traps and nets were made by twisting plant fibers and strips of inner bark.

The Indian bows and arrows were various shapes, depending upon the kind of wood used. Some bows were six feet high with very little curve. Shorter bows had more curve. The wide part of the bow was strengthened with strips of sinew.

Three-foot arrows were made of light straight wood or reed. Some tribes used arrows two feet long with tail feathers, and others used three. Sharp-tipped wooden arrows were used for small game and stone tips were used for large animals. Spears were usually about six feet long with a large stone tip, and the North-

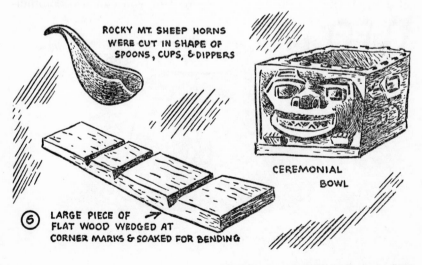

ROCKY MT. SHEEP HORNS
WERE CUT IN SHAPE OF
SPOONS, CUPS, & DIPPERS

CEREMONIAL
BOWL

6 LARGE PIECE OF
FLAT WOOD WEDGED AT
CORNER MARKS & SOAKED FOR BENDING

west Indians used harpoons with a thong or rope attached. The Indian tomahawk was used by the Algonquins.

One of the most interesting Northwest boxes or ceremonial bowls was made by forming all four sides from a single board. The board was cut partially through in three places and bent into a square after the wood had been made pliable by steaming. The two open ends were sewn together and then attached to the bottom piece with root stitches of cedar fiber, sunk in grooves or passed through holes. See Fig. 6. These were beautifully carved.

The Indian also used horn and clay for implements and utensils.

REFERENCES: Bureau of American Ethnology, *Bulletin 30*, pages 601-603. Stone-work: *Bulletin 30*, pages 638-643. Bone-work: *Bulletin 30*, pages 159-160.

BIRCH BARK

The Indians used birch bark to cover their dwellings, for containers, making canoes, moose callers, cups, combs, boxes, floats for fish nets and cut-out patterns.

How to Make a Birch Bark Basket: A simple small basket is illustrated in Fig. 7. Sew it together with thin strips of spruce root, using an awl or a large darning needle to punch the hole.

How to Decorate Your Basket: Applique (sew) small cut-out Indian patterns from other pieces of bark. The most common method of decorating birch bark is to scrape the design. You can also stitch the design with spruce root or you can use commer-mercial raffia.

BIRCHBARK FANS

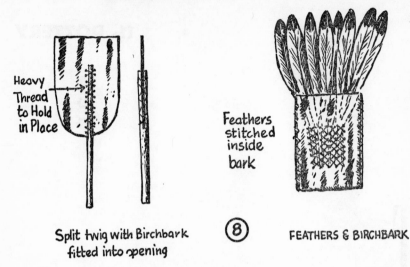

Heavy Thread to Hold in Place

Split twig with Birchbark fitted into opening

(8)

Feathers stitched inside bark

FEATHERS & BIRCHBARK

How to Make a Birch Bark Fan: Fig. 8 illustrates two kinds of Indian fans. One is made with a piece of birch bark with a stick handle split half way for inserting the fan and stitched with bark thong or heavy thread. The feather fan has a piece of folded birch bark for the handle. The feathers are spaced inside the folded bark and stitched in place with bark thong or heavy thread.

11. POTTERY

THE pottery of the southwest Indian was made by coiling a long rope of clay, layer on layer, until the shaping of the vessel had been completed.

HOW TO MOULD A PIECE OF POTTERY

Indian Materials You Can Use: If you live near a natural clay pit, you are all set, or you may have to use regular dry modeling clay.

Substitute Materials: Clay in powdered or moist form may be purchased from craft supply houses and local outlets. Craft supply houses also sell a self-hardening clay that does not have to be fired. Dextrin has been added to the clay and the air hardens it after it has been modeled.

Tools and Equipment: Smooth board or surface for rolling the clay, large pan for mixing the clay, mixing stick or spoon, paint brush and paints.

Indian Decorations: Vegetable, berry or root dyes.

Substitute Decorations: Oil paints.

Instructions for Moulding a Piece of Clay Pottery:

Fig. 1 refers to mixing your clay with enough water and a little sand to produce a thick mixture. Then let it set until it dries out

1 CLAY MIXED WITH WATER TO
PRODUCE A "THICK-SOUP" MIXTURE
*Then let set until it dries out
to consistency of pie dough*

2 SEVERAL ROLLS OF ABOUT ½"
IN THICKNESS ARE NOW HAND
ROLLED ON FLAT BOARD or
SMOOTH TABLE TOP

to a consistency of pie dough. In Fig. 2 the clay is being rolled in ¼" rolls on a long board or flat surface.

Fig. 3 shows you how to mould a pat of clay for the base of your vessel.

Fig. 4 shows you how to mould the clay, coiling one layer on top of the other, shaping it as you go along. Be sure to keep your hands moist during this step. Also be sure that you have enough room in the center of your vessel to insert your hand and hold it against the inside, directly opposite from your hand on the outside, as you smooth and shape the vessel as shown in Fig. 5.

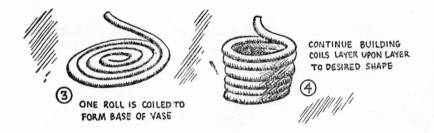

3 ONE ROLL IS COILED TO
FORM BASE OF VASE

CONTINUE BUILDING
COILS LAYER UPON LAYER
TO DESIRED SHAPE

4

Now moisten the vessel and smooth out any surface flaws, and you are ready to apply the "slip" (a thin mixture of clay and water) with a piece of cloth to the surface of the vessel; this will give it a final smooth polish.

Now you are ready to bake the vessel in an Indian kiln or oven.

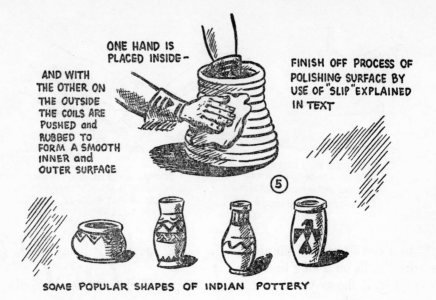

ONE HAND IS PLACED INSIDE —

AND WITH THE OTHER ON THE OUTSIDE THE COILS ARE PUSHED and RUBBED TO FORM A SMOOTH INNER and OUTER SURFACE

FINISH OFF PROCESS OF POLISHING SURFACE BY USE OF "SLIP" EXPLAINED IN TEXT

⑤

SOME POPULAR SHAPES OF INDIAN POTTERY

HOW TO MAKE AN INDIAN KILN

Indian Materials You Will Need: Large flat stone to hold pottery, five large, flat stones to make the four sides and top of the kiln. Fire wood.

How to Make Indian Kiln: Fig. 6 shows you how to place your piece of pottery upside down on a flat stone.

Fig. 7 shows how to arrange four flat stones as a wall around the piece of pottery.

Fig. 8 shows how to place a flat stone on top of the four stones forming the sides to complete the kiln.

⑥ PLACE PIECE UPSIDE DOWN ON FLAT SLAB SOMEWHAT LARGER THAN WIDEST PART OF PIECE.

FOUR MORE FLAT STONES ARE THEN FITTED AROUND PIECE. ⑦

⑧ A FIFTH STONE
IS PLACED ON TOP
TO CLOSE THE BOX

Fig. 9 show how to build a fire around the kiln (Figs. 9 and 10) and keep it going for about four to six hours. Keep packing the hot coals against the sides of the kiln. Remove the piece of pottery after it has completely cooled.

Decorating Your Piece of Pottery: Turn to Chapter 4, How to Use Indian Symbols, Designs, and Motifs, and pick out your favorite designs. Then trace the outline on your piece of pottery with a paint brush and black paint, and fill in the figures with

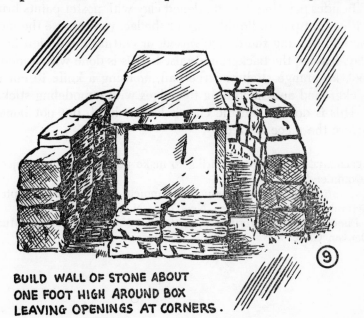

BUILD WALL OF STONE ABOUT
ONE FOOT HIGH AROUND BOX
LEAVING OPENINGS AT CORNERS.

⑨

FIRE IS THEN BUILT BETWEEN STONE WALL
and BOX. BUILD FIRE TO ABOUT $\frac{1}{2}$ WAY UP
SIDES OF BOX • FIRE SHOULD BE KEPT
GOING FOR ABOUT 6 HOURS, BEING CARE-
FUL TO KEEP HOT COALS AGAINST WALLS
OF BOX and ASHES WELL REMOVED.

colored oil paints to suit your taste. Be sure to let one color dry
before applying another.

Besides painting your hardened clay with poster paints brushed
with a transparent liquid glaze or shellac, you can use the incising
method, leaving the design raised, or cutting the design into the
clay, leaving the background raised. This is done with a modeling
tool, an orange stick or large nail, or using a knife to cut away
background and smoothing the edges with a modeling stick.

This is done when the clay is leather-hard, but not bone-dry,
before the piece is fired.

REFERENCES: For those desiring to make pottery a major project, we
recommend:
Creative Crafts for Campers, Hammett & Horrocks, Chapter IV,
Ceramics, Association Press, New York, N. Y.
Pueblo Indian Pottery Making, Leaflet No. 6, Denver Art Museum,
Denver, Colo.

12. GAMES AND SPORTS

INDIAN GAMES

THE Indians enjoyed fun, play, games, and sports, including a wide variety of foot and relay races, jumping, follow-the-leader, hide and seek, tag, shinny, hand and leg wrestling, tagtops, kickball, tug-of-war, marked stick games, stilts, archery, horse racing, swimming, and lacrosse, to mention just a few. In fact, it would be easier to list a group of games that were not enjoyed by the Indian men, women, boys, and girls.

Indian children played many games similar to the ones children play today. The girls played jack straws and "house" with dolls, and the boys made small bows and arrows and built small tipis, dance rattles, etc.

The Indian made use of the natural materials that surrounded him in making his game and sports equipment, including sticks and stones, pebbles, many kinds of seeds, bones, nuts, beads, leather, feathers, etc.

Here are a few games that involve simple handicraft:

Stick Games: A stick marked on one side with Indian designs is tossed in the air, each player scoring a point if it lands with the figure side up. Use a flat stick about one foot long, smooth down both sides and paint or carve Indian designs on one side only, as shown in Fig. 1. See Chapter 4, Indian Arts and Decorations, for Indian designs and symbols.

STICK GAME ①

Corn Cob Dart-and-Ball Game: Whittle a sharp point on the end of a lollipop stick or wooden meat skewer. Stick the other end into the core of a three inch long corn cob, attach a small feather at the other end of the cob. Make a ball about the size of a softball, using grass or cotton for the inside material and cover it with thin cloth. See Fig. 2.

The object of the game is to place the ball in the middle of a circle of players. Each player takes his turn trying to stick the ball, gaining one point every time he is successful.

CORN COB DART and BALL GAME

Snow Snake: The "snake" is a stick about 3 feet long and one inch thick. Smooth the underside with a knife or heavy-grade sandpaper. Carve one end in the shape of a snake's head, then paint or carve the body of the stick with marks suggesting the skin of a snake. See Fig. 3.

The game is played by skimming the snake over the hard ground or ice. The player making the snake glide the greatest distance, wins the point.

SNOW SNAKES

Kick Stick: Smooth down two sticks about one foot long and one inch thick. Carve or paint the sticks with Indian designs. See Fig. 4.

The object of the game is to have each player kick the stick around the council ring, with the first player returning to the starting point declared the winner.

KICK STICK

HIDDEN BALL GAME ⑤

Hidden-Ball Game: The general idea is to hide a small object, such as a bean or small stone, under one of four containers and having the opponent guess which container covers the object.

Four small baking powder cans make good covers. Decorate them with painted Indian designs. See Fig. 5.

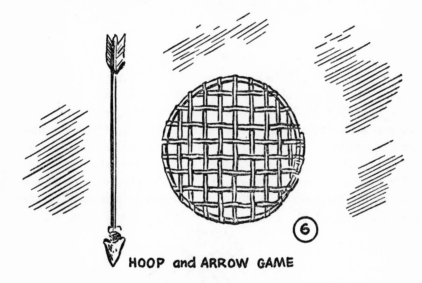

HOOP and ARROW GAME ⑥

Hoop and Arrow Game: Make an Indian hoop out of a young sapling, and make it pliable by soaking it in hot water. After you have shaved down the overlapping ends, lash them together with leather thong. Criss-cross the hoop with thong. You can substitute the lid of a large cheese box, cutting down the width of the band to ½ or 1 inch. See Fig. 6. One player gives his hoop a good roll, and his opponent tries to knock it over by hitting it with a thrown arrow or lance.

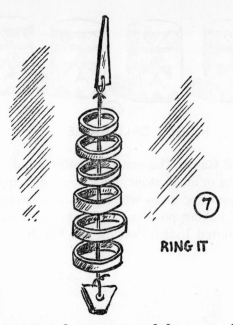

RING IT

Ring It: See Fig. 7. Indians originated the game of Ring It. Cut five or six roundsteak bones about one-fourth of an inch thick, and paint each a different color. A 30 inch string is tied to a stick, then run through all the bones but the last, to which the other end of the string is tied. Now all bones are placed on the stick, then tossed into the air. The idea of the game is to catch them all on the stick in one motion as they fall. The secret is to keep the bones lined up by pulling back down a little as they start to fall.

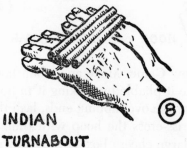

INDIAN TURNABOUT

Indian Turnabout: See Fig. 8. Indian children are expert in playing this game. Each player stands with his feet together. On the backs of his outstretched hands, which he holds close together, four light sticks or twigs about three inches long are placed. On the word "Go," each player tosses the twigs straight up into the air and twirls swiftly around without changing place. He then tries to catch the twigs on the palms of his two hands, held together, as they fall. Each player is given three tries, and the one who catches the most sticks is the winner.

ZIMBA

Zimba: The equipment for this game consists of a sharp-pointed stick attached to one end of a heavy cord or thong, and a ball of grass tied to the other end. The thong should be about 30 inches long. The game is played by holding the stick in the right hand with the point extending beyond the thumb and forefinger. The ball of grass on the opposite end of the cord or thong is thrown forward from the body and then jerked back. As it comes back, the player attempts to pierce the grass ball with the point of the stick. See Fig. 9.

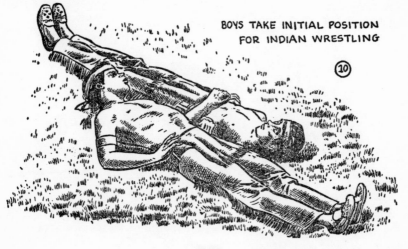

BOYS TAKE INITIAL POSITION
FOR INDIAN WRESTLING

Indian Wrestling: Big Wrestle—Fig. 10. Place two boys side by side, lying on their backs in opposite directions, each contestant's head opposite his opponent's buttocks. Inside elbows locked; outside hands on hips. On count of one and two each contestant lifts his left leg to vertical and returns it to floor, as practice and to get rhythm. On count of three, they hook ankles and attempt to roll the other over backward. The one rolled backward loses. Two out of three.

REFERENCE: *Games, Bulletin No. 30,* pages 483-486, Bureau of American Ethnology, Washington, D. C.

BIBLIOGRAPHY: *Indian Games,* Culin, Bureau of American Ethnology, Report, V, 24, 1902–3.

Workaday Life of the Pueblos, Ruth Underhill, Bureau of Indian affairs.

13. INDIAN DWELLINGS

THE Indians lived in dwellings ranging from crude lean-tos to apartment houses.

The climate and materials at hand largely determined the type of housing in various sections of the country.

In the northeast, the Indians built substantial rectangular houses with sides and ends formed of planks; in the forest regions, bark and mat houses; on the plains, the portable tipi. Cliffs in the dry areas provided flat slabs of stone, and the adobe houses were built of clay soil.

The majority of the western Indians lived in tipis. They were warm, dry, and easy to transport from place to place.

The Pawnees and Mandans built sod or dirt houses that could accommodate large families.

The Pueblo people had the most highly developed apartment houses.

The plains tipi was made out of a number of dressed buffalo skins, sewn together and supported by about 12 to 16 lodge poles. Some of the northern tribes covered their tipis with birch bark. Some of the plains Indians lived in dome-shaped earth lodges. Long strips of birch bark were stretched around the poles, layer on layer, one layer lapping over the other to shed the rain. The overlapping ends were sewn together with roots.

The Wichitas of Kansas and Oklahoma built beehive shaped dwellings out of prairie grass.

The hogans of the Navahos are made of brush, sticks, and mud.

The Iroquois Long House was covered with elm bark. The pole frames, posts, beams, and rafters were lashed together with the inner bark of the elm. The pieces of elm bark were laced on with inner bark. These large communal houses were divided into many compartments for a number of families. Similar bark-covered houses were made with a round roof.

The Seminoles made open sheltered grass thatched houses on stilts.

PLANK HOUSE of the NORTHWEST COAST TRIBES

The Indians of the Northwest Coast who lived around Puget Sound made their houses out of large cedar planks. These planks were split from the stately cedar tree, that grows to great size in the northwest. The framework or structure was made out of planks, about three feet wide and about eight inches thick. These planks were set upright in the ground, like poles about fifty feet apart. The uprights were about 12 to 14 feet apart, which made a living space for one family between the posts. Heavy beams were placed on top of the posts. Row of smaller beams were placed at right angles to the main beams.

This house had a gable roof with a center ridge pole. Planks of wood about 3 feet wide were laid in a double layer (much like tile) on the rows of small logs.

The wall planks were lashed with battens over the cracks and held in place with long strips, lashed to the inside. Sometimes the loose planks were wedged in place. The early houses had mats covering the doorways.

② GRASS or BRUSH HUT of
CALIFORNIA SEED GATHERERS

NOMAD HOGAN of SOUTHWEST

SOUTHWEST HOGANS

The Navaho Indians lived in an earth lodge called a hogan.

Some of them had a framework of three logs with forked tops, forming a tripod, with the legs facing north, south, and west. The tops were locked together and two logs were laid parallel on the east side from the apex to the ground, with a door frame set up where they reached the ground. Sticks and brush were then piled on the framework, and then covered with a layer of earth.

The doorway looked like a dormer window and was usually covered with a blanket. The center of the floor was dug out, forming a sort of ring-side circular earth bench.

Fig. 3 shows you how Navahos sometimes made their lodge with crossed log sidings, and the roof logs covered with brush, straw, and earth. A hole was left in the top for smoke to escape.

Some of the present-day Navahos still live in very primitive hogans made of poles, earth, and straw, and stoutly covered with a tarpaulin.

The Pueblo cliff dwellings were built on tops of mesas for protection from enemies. The cliff homes were made of adobe (a-do'bi). Adobe is a Spanish word meaning clay and straw bricks dried in the sun. In the dry climate of that region, buildings made of adobe last about as long as the ones made of oven-baked brick. See Fig. 4.

④ PUEBLO DWELLINGS
of SOUTHWEST INDIANS

Adobe bricks were laid the same as regular bricks. Heavy beams were first laid across the brick walls to form the roof of the first story, then thin poles or brush were laid the opposite way across the beams. The cracks and crevices were filled with a layer of clay, thus making the ceiling for one story and the floor for another. Each story was made narrower than the one below it. Each story had a small platform all around it, like a porch without a roof.

The early adobe houses had no doors in the first floor. They used ladders to get into their homes, and they let themselves in through an opening in the ceiling. In times of danger, they climbed up the ladders and pulled them up so no enemy could get inside. The early adobe homes had small holes for windows covered with a transparent stone or selenite, and an opening for a door above the first floor. Now adobe houses have glass windows and conventional doors on all floors.

Probably the best known type of Indian dwelling is the Southwest apartment house called the Pueblo. These homes were built like the Pueblo cliff dwellings out of adobe brick, mud, stone, or a combination of all three.

Each section or floor belongs to one clan and each family has several rooms on that floor. The largest rooms, which are the living rooms, have a three cornered fireplace next to the door.

A very interesting scale model Pueblo village can be made by covering shoe boxes with clay, mud, or using brown paint. Taffy sticks or toothpicks can be used to make the ladders.

THE PLAINS TIPI

The Plains Indian lived in a conical tent called a Tipi (tee-pee) which is a Sioux word applied to tents. "Ti" means "dwelling" and "Pi" means "used for," but each tribe had its own name for the tipi.

The early covering was made of dressed cow buffalo hides, until the destruction of the herds. Since then canvas has been used. The size of the early cover depended upon the wealth of the family.

Since canvas tipi is mighty expensive and very difficult to make, and because there are so many other kinds of interesting Indian dwellings, we suggest the wigwam and bark, grass or brush hut as an excellent and easy-to-make dwelling for the individual craftsman or as a camp project.

However, we will give a brief description of the major steps in making a tipi.

The poles can be made of lodge-pole pine, cedar, spruce, and some other straight, slim trees. They average about 25 feet in length, although some are as long as 40 feet, depending on the size of the canvas.

THE PLAINS TIPI

The poles are tied together at their crossing with a rope or rawhide in tripod fashion, as shown in Fig. 6. The poles are raised and put in position (Fig. 7), leaving enough space between two poles for the opening. You can use 20 or 25 poles.

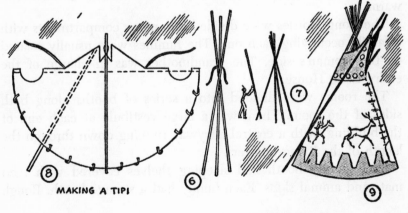

MAKING A TIPI

The canvas cover is laid out in Fig. 8. For a twelve-footer, you will need 32 yards of 6-ounce duck, or heavier. Cut it into strips of 8 yards long and sew them together into a 4 x 8 yard rectangle.

When all the poles but one are in place, this pole is tied to a tongue on top of the cover and raised, as shown in Fig. 9. A guy rope is used to help raise the cover. Then the two sides for the cover are pulled around the poles until they meet in front. One end of the cover is laid over the other and pinned together with foot long wooden sticks, one above the other, about 6 inches apart. When all is tight, the cover is staked to the ground, as shown in Fig. 5. Use semi-thick oil paints for the designs.

REFERENCE: *The Plains Indian Tipi.* Leaflet No. 19, Denver Art Museum, Denver, Colo.

BIBLIOGRAPHY: *The Indian Tipi. Its History, Construction, and Use.* Reginald and Gladys Laubin. Univ. of Oklahoma Press, 1957. 208 pages.

THE IROQUOIS LONG HOUSE

The Iroquois of New York made long communal houses, Fig. 10, covered with elm bark, which were called Long Houses. They looked like huge, one-story barns. The frames were sturdily built of crotched posts with beams and rafters lashed together with the inner bark of the elm. Squares of bark tied together like shingles were put over the frame of logs. The early Long Houses had no windows. The only light came through the openings in the roof and the doors at each end, then during the winter or cold months the doors were covered with skins to keep the houses warm.

The Long Houses were divided into many compartments with a family occupying each one. The families were usually related on the woman's side. The grandmother was in charge of the entire Long House.

The rooms were divided into a series of booths along both sides of the room. There was a large vestibule at each end of the building, with a central alleyway running down through the length of the living quarters.

Each family booth had sleeping shelves covered with reed mats and animal skins. Each family had a storage booth. Rough

LONG HOUSE of IROQUOIS

stone fireplaces were located along the central alleyway, with a fire for each pair of booths.

Up to about 1800, it was the general custom to serve one meal a day in the middle of the morning, although the food pots were simmering all day, so that anyone could snack when he felt like it.

REFERENCE: *The Iroquois Long House,* Leaflet No. 12, Denver Art Museum, Denver, Colo.

SEMINOLE CHICKEES

The Florida Seminole Indians lived in a warm, moist climate and swampy land, and that is why they built their homes (called chickees) high above the ground.

As you can see in Fig. 11, they built a sloping roof of palmetto fronds to shed the rains. Each chickee usually housed a single family.

The chickee had no side walls.

The Seminoles had to be very careful with fire, and, therefore, several families joined together in sharing one cooking hut.

SEMINOLE CHICKEE

BED PLATFORM

GREAT LAKES AND EASTWARD WIGWAM
AND
CALIFORNIA GRASS OR BRUSH HUT

Figs. 13-17 show how to build a framework of poles for a grass or bark wigwam. They are not difficult to build and can be made quite attractive and comfortable for a Boy Scout or YMCA camp. They can be made round or slightly oblong in shape, about 10 or 12 feet in diameter.

Secure 8 or 10 slim saplings about 3 inches at the base and a number of smaller ones for the circular supports. Stick the base of each pole in the ground, then bend it and ram the other end

GREAT LAKES WIGWAM

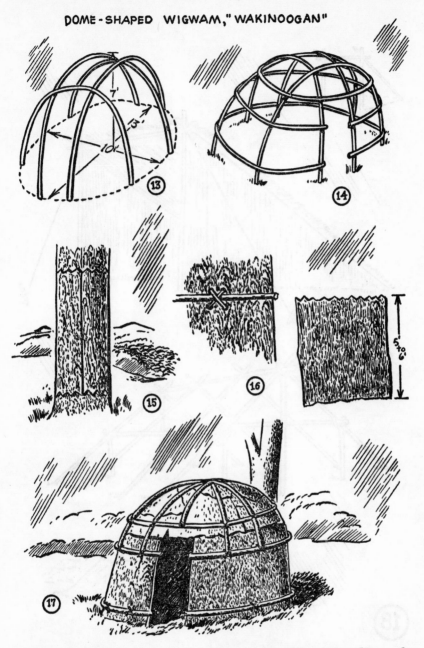

of the pole in the ground a similar depth (Fig. 13). Then split some saplings and lash them around the frame with strips of basswood bark, leather thong, or heavy cord as in Fig. 14.

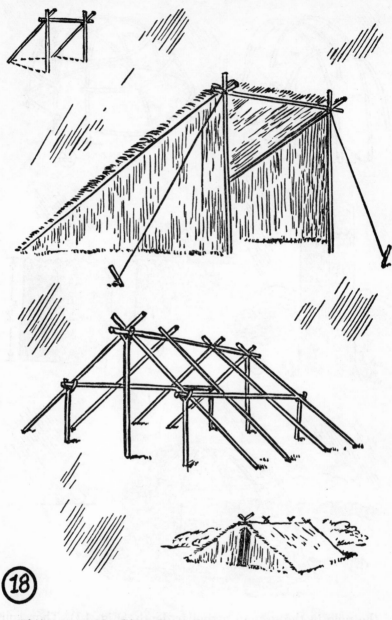

TWO TYPES OF DENS EASILY CONSTRUCTED

18

Now you are ready to apply the bark or grass. A WORD OF CAUTION: Be careful about stripping the bark without the owner's consent. Perhaps you can find a large fallen tree in your camp woods or secure one from a saw mill.

White cedar bark is the best and second best would be basswood, elm, hemlock, spruce, ash or cottonwood.

Be sure to select a large tree. Cut the bark as illustrated in Fig. 15, using a hand axe as high as you can reach if the tree is standing.

Set the bark strips around the frame work and lash down with split saplings as shown in Fig. 17. Cut small holes in the bark and lash the outside saplings to the inside frame saplings as shown in Fig. 16. Now lash the strips of ceiling bark to the saplings in the same manner.

If birch bark is available, it can be used to cover the roof for complete water-proofing. Secure the strips of birch bark with long strips of bark rope.

Leave a small opening in the top to let the smoke out. This can be covered with a piece of bark in rainy weather. A large piece of bark can be used for a door.

The California Seed Gatherers brush hut had the same general frame structure as the eastern wigwam, but because of their milder climate, they substituted boughs, brush and long grasses for the bark covering (see Fig. 2). The grass thatch is laid in layers, beginning at the ground and tied to the frame.

A cool summer den for camp can be made by using boughs, brush and tall grasses as shown in Fig. 18.

INDIAN FURNITURE

There was very little Indian furniture as we know it, because life in the Indian home was very simple. The type of dwelling had a lot to do with the kind of furniture it contained. For instance, the furnishings in the tipi differed from that in the communal houses. In most dwellings the seating arrangement was along the walls. Mats of woven bark and rushes were used in many dwellings. Pillows were made with skins stuffed with feathers, animal hair, or Spanish moss. The bearskin was often the seat of honor. The pueblos had seats of stone or rectangular stools made

CHIPPEWA BED FRAME

from a single block of wood, in addition to a masonry bench extending all or partly around the room. The Northwest coast had long settees facing the fire against the partitions that divided the family space in the communal houses. Stationary couches served as seats in the daytime and as beds at night. They were arranged against the walls in the earth lodges. The Plains Indians used a couch consisting of a mat of willows stretched upon a low platform with its tapering ends raised and fastened to tripods which formed the head and footboards. A buffalo skin was fitted to the bed and served as a mattress.

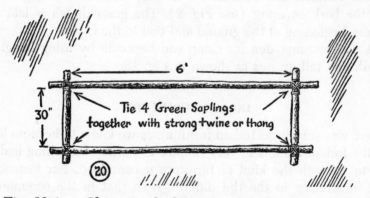

Fig. 19 is a Chippewa bed frame. Fig. 20 clearly illustrates the simple construction of the bed frame, using four strong, straight saplings lashed together with leather thong or heavy cord. Figs. 21 and 22 show you how to cover the frame with a piece of heavy canvas.

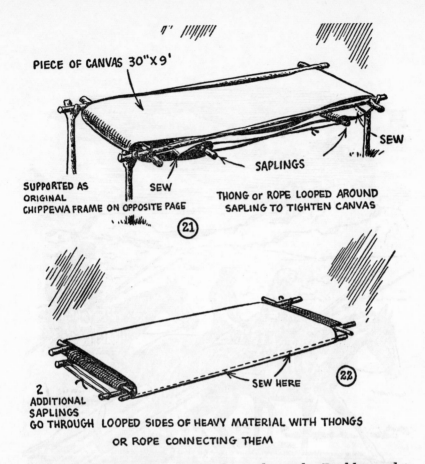

PIECE OF CANVAS 30"X 9'

SEW

SAPLINGS

SUPPORTED AS
ORIGINAL
CHIPPEWA FRAME ON OPPOSITE PAGE

SEW

THONG or ROPE LOOPED AROUND
SAPLING TO TIGHTEN CANVAS

㉑

㉒

SEW HERE

2
ADDITIONAL
SAPLINGS
GO THROUGH LOOPED SIDES OF HEAVY MATERIAL WITH THONGS
OR ROPE CONNECTING THEM

Wall decorations were confined mostly to the Pueblos and to the North Pacific Coast homes. Colorful shields, weapons, ceremonial equipment, and blankets added color to the interior of the Plains dwellings.

EXCELLENT REFERENCE: Bureau of American Ethnology, *Bulletin 30*, pages 476 and 477.

14. INDIAN TRANSPORTATION

INDIAN TRANSPORTATION

THE Indian used the travois in the south, the sledge in the north for land travel, and the canoe for waterways. He also invented and perfected the toboggan and snowshoes.

The sledge was used only when the ground was snow-covered. In early times both sledge and travois were drawn by dogs (see Fig. 2); but as soon as horses were obtained, the dogs were freed from the travois, and horses drew the loads. The travois was used by the Plains Indian to transport his possessions, and it is only recently that he exchanged it for a wagon.

THE TRAVOIS

Travois is a French trapper word, perhaps a corruption of "travers" or "a travers" (across), referring to the crossing of the poles over the horse's withers.

The travois consists of two poles about the size of lodge poles, crossed near their smaller ends, and held in place toward the larger end by crosspieces three feet apart. The space between these two cross braces is occupied by a stiff rawhide netting running from one pole to the other, and strong enough to carry a weight of several hundred pounds (shown in Fig. 1). The crossed ends of the poles are placed just at the front of the saddle, and the separated braced ends drag upon the ground

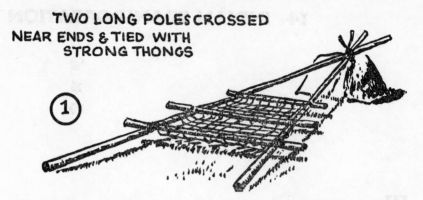

TWO LONG POLES CROSSED
NEAR ENDS & TIED WITH
STRONG THONGS

behind. Bearing a part of the weight on his shoulders, the horse drags the contrivance and its load over the rough prairie and along narrow mountain trails with rarely a mishap (see Fig. 3). On the platform of the travois are carried loads of meat from the buffalo-killing, the various possessions of the owner in moving camp from place to place, a sick or wounded individual too weak to ride, and sometimes a wickerwork cage in which are confined

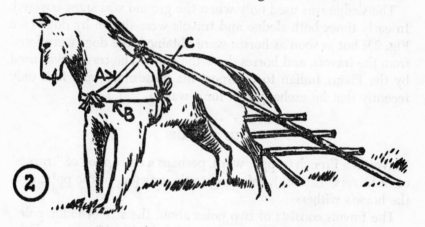

TRAVOIS HARNESS SHOWING
COLLAR (A) BREAST BAND (B) AND
SHOULDER BAND (C)

TRAVOIS WITH HORSE CARRYING PAPOOSE

small children or even a family of tiny puppies with their mother. Things that cannot be conveniently packed on the backs of the horses are put upon the travois. Sometimes the travois bears the dead, for with certain tribes it is essential to the future well-being of the departed that they be brought back to the tribal burying ground near the village.

BARK CANOES

The Indians used two kinds of canoes. One was made with elm or birch bark and the other, a dugout, was hollowed out of a log, usually white cedar.

The elm-bark canoe was made by stripping off the bark in a single piece. Sometimes the strips were sewed together with a cord of twisted bark. This was bent inside out, so that the out-

BIRCH BARK CANOE

side of the canoe was formed of the outside bark, and was then fitted over a rigid frame of poles. The ends were shaped and brought together and sewed with long fiber roots, by means of a bone awl or needle. The gunwale was strengthened by strips of hard wood, sewn to the bark with roots or cedar bark and fastened together at each end of the boat. The boat was strengthened with ribs of hard wood from one gunwale to the other and with long strips for the flooring and sides. The seams and cracks were pitched with spruce gum or pine pitch.

Even more handsome than the elm bark canoes were the famed birch bark canoes. These were made by the Algonquin tribes. The birch bark canoes were made in the same way as those of the elm bark.

These bark canoes were light. If a river became impassable, a man lifted his canoe on his shoulders and carried it to the next river or lake. Then he put it back into the water and paddled away. (See Fig. 4.)

Bark canoes are extremely difficult to handle by one who is not accustomed to them, and turn over on the slightest provocation.

DUGOUTS

Dugouts were not so graceful or so light as bark canoes, but they were sturdier and more durable. Late in the fall, men cut down trees and let them season for the winter. In spring they rolled the logs (usually white cedar) to the water's edge, where they planned to make the dugouts.

On the nearby beach the Indians built large fires. Then they threw the embers from the fire on the logs, making sure that they burned evenly and slowly into the wood. As the wood charred, they used a sharp stone, a large sharp bone, or a primitive chisel and wooden hammer and carefully chipped and scraped out the inside and outside until completed. In this slow way they dug out each log. The Indians were so skillful that the walls of a dugout were often only an inch thick.

The dugout is then braced by two or more crosspieces, which are sewed to the gunwales with steamed cedar twigs on either side so that the vessel cannot spread. The painting follows,

⑤ TOPVIEW OF SEMINOLE INDIANS
DUGOUT SHOWING GRACEFUL
LINES OF CRAFT

and the vessel is ready for use. Only seasoned and perfect timber is used for these canoes. (See Fig. 5.)

Some of the large canoes carried a sail.

The shape of the bow and stern and the decorations differed from tribe to tribe as shown in Fig. 6, a Tlingit dugout.

In such canoes the Indians of the North Pacific make long journeys over the open seas, facing rough weather, and capturing sea otters, seals, sea lions, and whales. The larger canoes were used to carry war parties, and the sudden appearance of one of these great boats full of fighting men carried consternation to the hearts of the dwellers in the village that it threatened.

Whether in a dugout or a bark canoe, a man used a carved wooden paddle.

The Seminole Indians of Florida made the most graceful dugouts. The Seminole were skillful sailors, with ample practice in Florida's swamps where they lived. Standing in their canoes, men and boys were able to spear fish and alligators. This called for great skill and perfect balance.

⑥ TLINGIT DUGOUT

(7)

THE BULL-BOAT

A boat used by the Indian women of the Sioux, Mandan, Arikara, and Hidatsa tribes, particularly on the Missouri River, was known as the bull-boat.

It was a tub-shaped vessel of willow frame covered with rawhide.

The women used it to carry their goods down or across the rivers. It was so light that when one was emptied, a woman could take it on her back and make her way across the land. See Fig. 7.

(8)

BALSA BOAT

In California, the Indians used a tule balsa boat, made from rushes tied in bundles.

It was shaped more or less like a cigar. See Fig. 8.

A step-by-step construction outline for making an Indian sled is shown in Figures 9, 10, and 11.

Indian Materials You Will Need: Secure a straight, sturdy, green maple or ash sapling about 15 feet long, and at least 5 inches in diameter at the base; it must have four strong limbs growing from two sides of the trunk, as shown in Fig. 9. Or find two saplings with four strong limbs in line on one side of the trunk. You will need 10 sturdy braces about 28″ long and 1″ thick, for lashing the runners together and additional bracing, as shown in Fig. 11. You will need two braces for the back rest frame about 38″ long. You will need 15 braces about 28″ long for the seat, as shown in Fig. 12, and about 50 feet of leather thong, ¼″ thick, for lashing the braces.

Substitute Materials: You will need a strip of heavy canvas about 22″ wide and long enough to cover the seat and back rest,

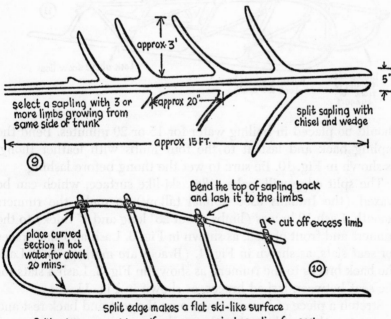

approx. 3′

5″

select a sapling with 3 or more limbs growing from same side of trunk

approx 20″

split sapling with chisel and wedge

approx 15 FT.

⑨

Bend the top of sapling back and lash it to the limbs

cut off excess limb

place curved section in hot water for about 20 mins.

⑩

split edge makes a flat ski-like surface

Split edge can end here if one uses a single sapling for each runner. In this case splitting should be done by cutting into the sapling at this point rather than from end.

as shown in Fig. 12, and about 20 one-half inch grommets for lacing the canvas together, as shown in Fig. 4.

Tools and Equipment You Will Need: Hammer, chisel, wedge, 20 one-half inch grommets, saw, and rule.

How to Make the Sled: After you have split down the center, using a chisel and wedge, as shown in Fig. 9, the curved parts

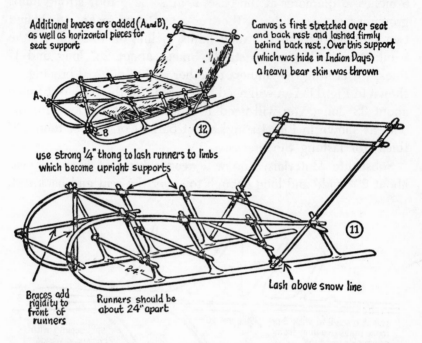

Additional braces are added (A and B), as well as horizontal pieces for seat support

Canvas is first stretched over seat and back rest and lashed firmly behind back rest. Over this support (which was hide in Indian Days) a heavy bear skin was thrown

use strong ¼" thong to lash runners to limbs which become upright supports

Braces add rigidity to front of runners

Runners should be about 24" apart

Lash above snow line

should be placed in boiling water for 15 or 20 minutes. Bend the sapling back and lash it to the four limbs with leather thong, as shown in Fig. 10. Be sure to wet the thong before lashing.

The split edge will make a flat, ski-like surface, which can be waxed (the Indians used animal tallow) to make the runners smooth. Lash 10 braces (limbs about 28" long and 1" thick) to the runners and front of sled, as shown in Fig. 3. Lash also slat braces for seat slats, as shown in Fig. 4. (Braces are marked "B.") Lash the back braces to the runners, as shown in Fig. 3. Lash 4 slats for the seat between lashed braces, as shown in Fig. 11.

Stretch a piece of heavy canvas over the seat and back rest and lace it together with leather thong (be sure to use ½" grommets) behind the back rest, as shown in Fig. 12.

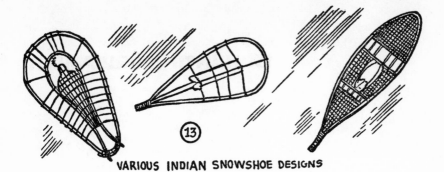

VARIOUS INDIAN SNOWSHOE DESIGNS

INDIAN SNOWSHOES

The first snowshoes were made by the Indians. They were crude, webfooted affairs. The Indians of Maine and Canada continue to fashion the finest models today. Present day snowshoes are constructed along the same general lines, although the types of frames differ considerably in size and shape.

The simple, early-type Indian snowshoes were made by bending ash, beech or willow boughs into crude shaped shoes, as shown in Fig. 13. The frames should be steamed in hot water before bending them into the desired shape.

The Indians laced the inside of the shoe frame with strips of wet leather thong, insuring a tight, snug fit.

A simple leather stirrup for the toe and instep, and a heel strap were added. The shoes were quickly taken off by pushing the heel strap down.

Since space does not permit a complete, detailed outline for making a modern-day pair of snowshoes, we refer the reader to two excellent articles on snowshoe-making in the "What to Do and How to Do It" book, edited by D. C. Beard and published by Scribner's, New York. Most public libraries have this book.

––––––

(We wish to acknowledge the technical assistance of Irwin Brambley in preparing the section on the "Indian Sled.")

INDIAN HUNTING AND HUNTING EQUIPMENT

"AN INDIAN is next to a bloodhound in his ability to follow a track."

John Witthoft, Pennsylvania State Anthropologist, in his Pennsylvania Historical and Museum Commission, No. 6, THE AMERICAN INDIAN AS HUNTER, tells us that both the mental attitudes of the Indian hunter and his hunting techniques have almost completely disappeared, except in a few areas, and it is now very difficult to get full information on either from living people.

Indians washed themselves clean before going on the hunt so the animals could not smell them.

We do know that deer were taken by still-hunting and stalking, by driving, and by snares. In stalking, the Indian would imitate the bleat of a lost fawn to attract the deer. Sometimes they would surround a large herd of deer and drive them into a bottleneck, where they would be killed by a small group of the hunting party. Buffaloes were caught by impounding them in a V-shaped pile of brush and stones at the edge of a cliff. The herd was worked into the V, and driven over the cliff and into a corral, where the animals were killed.

They would use spring pole snares, made by pegging down the bottom of a large noose in a game-trail, attaching the rope to a

bent-over sapling. Witthoft tells us that some of our early pilgrim fathers would blunder into a group of such deer snares and be yanked off the ground, perhaps to the great amusement of their Indian neighbors. Log falls were built for coyotes, foxes, and wolves. A hole was cut in the ice over the entrance to a beaver lodge, and then rods were driven into the lodge to drive the beaver out. They were speared as they swam out of the entry. Perhaps it is needless to say that this is illegal today. (In passing, we would like to say that we consider the steel trap a vicious invention. Fur-bearing animals should be raised for the market on fur farms.) Wild turkeys were taken by the use of the bow and by trapping.

Eagles were caught by hand with the hunter crouched in a pit under brush covers. The hunter caught the eagle by the legs if it alighted for the bait.

Indians used the bow, the beaver-spear, the blowgun, the fish hook, and the fish-spear. Indian fishing involved fish traps, pounds, and fish poisons, more than did fishing with the line or fish-gig.

Indian hunting was closely involved with ritual and religious concepts.

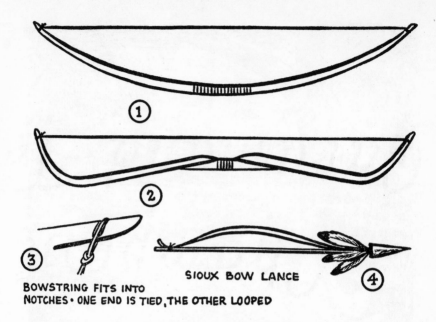

BOWSTRING FITS INTO
NOTCHES • ONE END IS TIED, THE OTHER LOOPED

SIOUX BOW LANCE

BOWS AND ARROWS

The Encyclopedia Britannica ranks the bow and arrow with fire and speech as the three most important advances in mankind's history. It was man's first harnessing of energy.

Indian bows and arrows varied greatly in size, form, material, workmanship, power, and efficiency.

Most North American tribes preferred short, broad bows of flat section, and short, heavy, well-feathered arrows.

Indians reinforced their bows with sinew or rawhide, and used sinew or rawhide bowstrings. Sometimes the bowstring was made of twisted fiber plant.

There was a great variety of arrowheads. Each tribe knew how to make heads or tips which were best adapted to kill the game in their hunting areas. Long, sharp-edged, lance-like heads were used for killing large game. Small, blunt heads of wood were used for knocking down birds and small game.

Some bows are made with one piece of wood (Fig. 1) and some are pieced together with wood, horn, and bone (Fig. 2). One end of the bowstring fits into the notch (Fig. 3) and the other end is looped. Fig. 4 is a Sioux combination bow and lance. Fig. 5 shows how thongs of leather or sinew are used to bind arrowheads to the

shaft. Flint, bone, and wood arrowheads are shown in Fig. 6. Fig. 7 shows the three parts of an arrow; namely, the head, shaft, and feather. The Plains Indians used a long feather, and the Northern Indians used a short feather (Fig. 8). Quivers and bows (Fig. 9) were made from skins and hides and were sometimes highly decorated.

Some Indians used two tail feathers, and some used a set of three.

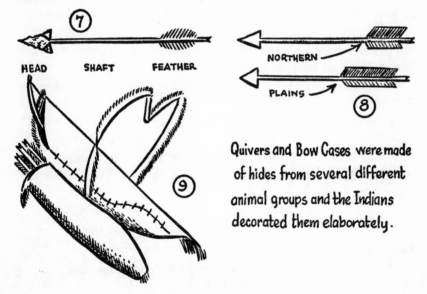

Quivers and Bow Cases were made of hides from several different animal groups and the Indians decorated them elaborately.

THE FLAT BOW

Through mathematical analysis, laboratory tests, high-speed photography and field tests, it was discovered that the famous English long bow does not have the most efficient shape. Its rounded limbs are beautiful, but experts have found that the simple plain rectangle cross section, or American flat bow, is the better.

HOW TO MAKE A FLAT BOW

Indian Materials You Can Use: The Indian used the most available wood to make his bow. Many kinds of wood will serve for a bow, but only a few are good for bow making. In their order of excellence, they are yew, Tennessee red cedar (backed with hickory), lemonwood, Osage orange, lancewood, and second-growth white hickory. Indians also used ash, choke berry, and willow. For the beginner, we recommend hickory, which can be obtained in almost any hardwood dealer's stock. If possible, try to get air-seasoned wood.

Substitute Materials: Archery supply houses sell lemonwood bow kits in rough stave or cut to approximate outline. When you order your bow, be sure to ask for a wide stave for a flat bow.

Tools and Equipment You Will Need: Measuring tape, marking pencil, sharp knife, or other cutting tool, small plane, rawhide bowstring, and friction tape.

Instructions for Making Bow: Secure a piece of mill cut wood (air-seasoned yew, red cedar, or hickory) 2 x 2 x 5 feet (Fig. 10).

Draw outline of bow (front) on one side, as shown in Fig. 11, and draw outline of bow (side) as shown in Fig. 12. Very carefully and slowly carve front and side of bow. Cut notch at each end for bowstring. When carving is completed, smooth all surfaces with sandpaper.

Wrap grip area with rawhide or friction tape as in Fig. 13.

When you have finished shaping the bow and have wrapped the grip area, give the entire bow a coat of shellac.

String your bowstring, as shown in Fig. 14, by tying it firmly at one end, leaving a small loop to hang the bow, and making a loop at the other end for slipping it into the notch. Refer to Fig. 15 for proper manner of stringing the bow. Fig. 16 shows proper manner of hanging up your bow.

Fig. 17 shows an easy-to-make quiver to hold your arrows. It can be made of leather, plastic, canvas, or cloth.

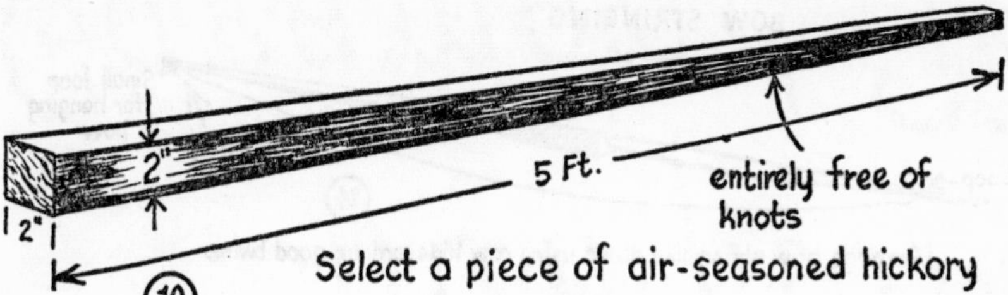

2"

2"

5 Ft.

entirely free of knots

Select a piece of air-seasoned hickory

(10)

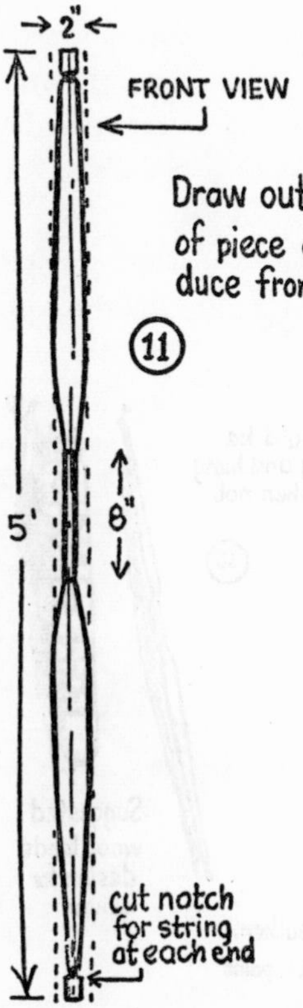

→ 2" ←

FRONT VIEW

Draw outline on one side of piece and carve to produce front view of bow

(11)

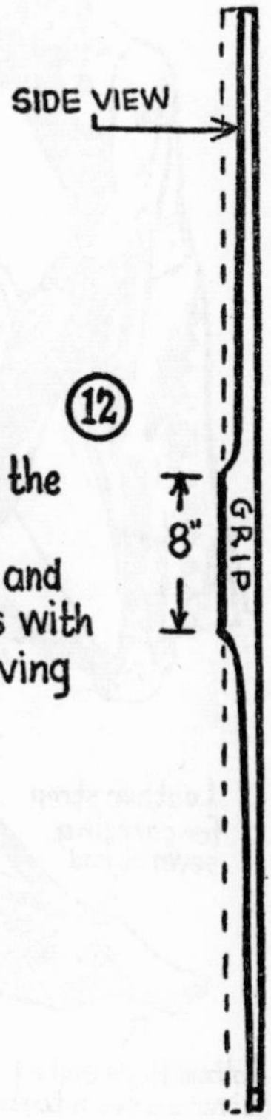

SIDE VIEW

(12)

Draw and carve out the side view of bow. Round off all edges and smooth all surfaces with sandpaper after carving

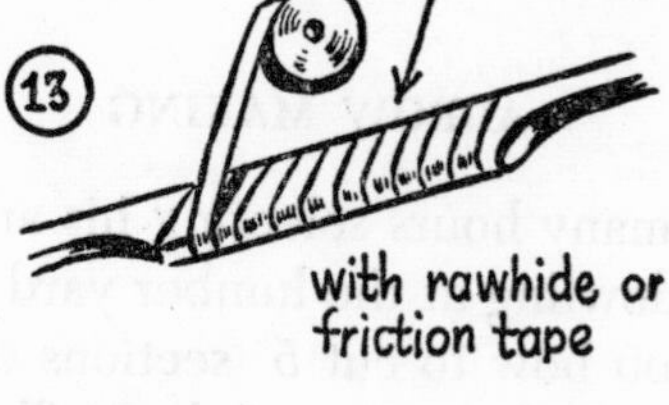

5'

6"

8"

GRIP

cut notch for string at each end

Wrap grip area

(13)

with rawhide or friction tape

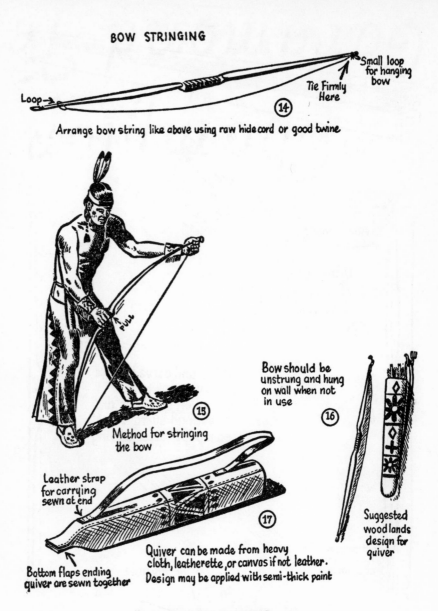

Small loop
for hanging
bow

Tie Firmly
Here

Loop →

(14)

Arrange bow string like above using raw hide cord or good twine

PULL

Method for stringing
the bow

(15)

Bow should be
unstrung and hung
on wall when not
in use

(16)

Suggested
woodlands
design for
quiver

Leather strap
for carrying
sewn at end

(17)

Bottom flaps ending
quiver are sewn together

Quiver can be made from heavy
cloth, leatherette, or canvas if not leather.
Design may be applied with semi-thick paint

ARROW MAKING

The Indian spent many hours selecting his arrow shafts, but you can secure ¼ inch dowling at the lumber yard (Fig. 18).

Fig. 19 shows you how to cut 5″ sections of turkey or chicken feathers. Slice through the center of the quill.

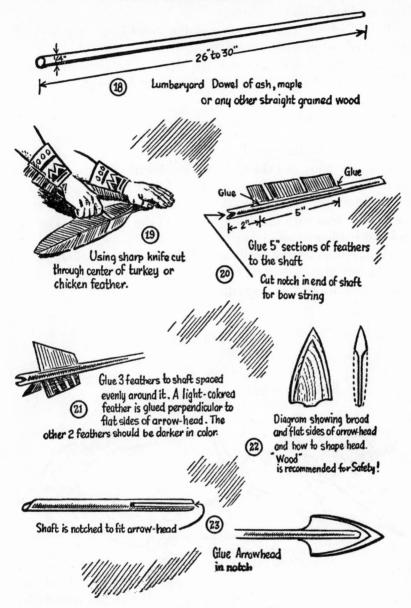

18. Lumberyard Dowel of ash, maple or any other straight grained wood

26" to 30"

¼"

19. Using sharp knife cut through center of turkey or chicken feather.

20. Glue 5" sections of feathers to the shaft

Glue

Glue

2" — 5"

Cut notch in end of shaft for bow string

21. Glue 3 feathers to shaft spaced evenly around it. A light-colored feather is glued perpendicular to flat sides of arrow-head. The other 2 feathers should be darker in color.

22. Diagram showing broad and flat sides of arrow-head and how to shape head. "Wood" is recommended for Safety!

Shaft is notched to fit arrow-head

23. Glue Arrowhead in notch

Glue feather to shaft, as shown in Fig. 20.

Fig. 21 shows you how to glue three feathers to the shaft, spacing them evenly around it. The lighter colored feather should be glued perpendicular to the flat side of the arrow, and the other two feathers should be darker.

Fig. 22 shows the side view of the arrowhead, which should be carved out of wood for safety.

Fig. 23 shows how to notch the shaft to hold the arrowhead. Glue the inserted part of the arrowhead in the notch.

LOAD—AIM—SHOOT

Figs. 24 and 25 show you how to hold the bow and arrow. While loading, be sure to hold the bow level with the ground—never load with the bow in firing position. Fig. 25 shows you how to hold the arrow lightly between the first two fingers. The arrow lies on the bow with the notch straddling the bowstring. The dark colored feather should be up, as shown in Fig. 26.

Fig. 27 shows firing position with the right hand along side of cheek; left arm fully extended with the bow drawn across the chest, and the feet well apart.

ARCHERY

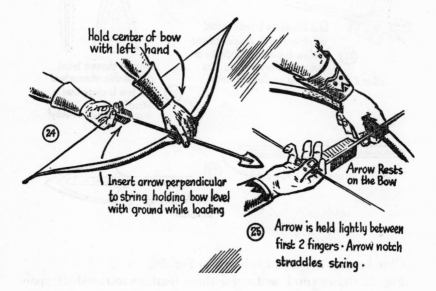

Hold center of bow with left hand

Insert arrow perpendicular to string holding bow level with ground while loading

Arrow Rests on the Bow

Arrow is held lightly between first 2 fingers · Arrow notch straddles string .

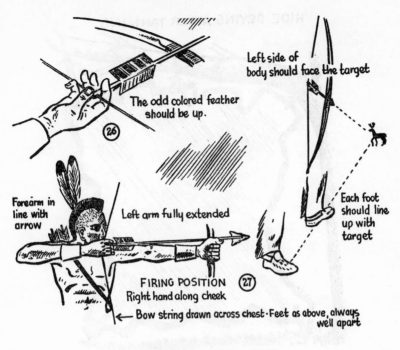

The odd colored feather should be up.

26

Left side of body should face the target

Forearm in line with arrow

Left arm fully extended

Each foot should line up with target

FIRING POSITION 27
Right hand along cheek

← Bow string drawn across chest · Feet as above, always well apart

TANNING A SMALL SKIN
(*Squirrel, raccoon, rabbit*)

Tanning a large skin takes much time and patience. As a beginner, you might like to tan a small animal skin, using a combination of the Indian method and some tricks of the white man.

Step 1: Scrape off all the flesh, fat, and blood.

Step 2: Soak the hide in salt water (half and half: 1 gal. of water to 1 pound of salt) for about 4 or 5 hours.

Step 3: Drain off the salt and rub salt into the flesh side. Fold the skin, flesh side to flesh side, roll it into a bundle, and let the salt work over night.

Step 4: Now give the skin a final scraping and cleaning, using a dull-edged tool, such as the wooden handle of a putty knife. When you have finished this job, dry the skin in a shady spot.

Step 5: Now use the white man's method of tanning the skin by soaking the hide in a solution of alum, salt, and water, mixing 1 lb. of alum in some hot water in one pan, and 2½ lb. of salt in 5 gal. of water in another pan. Combine the two solutions and mix until both chemicals are thoroughly dissolved.

Hunting Equipment / 227

Let the hide soak for about two or three days, not forgetting to stir the solution and skin two or three times a day.

Step 6: Drain the skin and thoroughly rinse it in water for 10 or 15 minutes. The Indians used to place the hide in a stream, fastened down with rocks or wooden pegs, to free the skin completely of the salt.

Step 7: Then, like the Indian, hang the skin up to dry for a day.

Step 8: Dampen the skin and, like the Indian, pull and stretch it in all directions.

Step 9: Knead some warm lard or butter into the skin. The Indian used a mixture of animal brains, liver, fats, and some vegetable broths.

Step 10: Sometimes the Indian smoked the skin over dampened green hardwood to make it waterproof and dry quickly after a rain.

BIBLIOGRAPHY: *Leaflet No. 2, Dept. of Indian Art,* Denver Art Museum, Denver, Colorado.

Tan Your Own Hide, William A. Burns, Science Guide No. 45, The American Museum of Natural History, New York, N. Y.

POSTSCRIPT

THE AMERICAN INDIAN

He came quietly, in the dawn of history. Here, long centuries before the white man sought his freedom on these shores, he built his own credo: He believed first in the rights of the individual . . . and in his great dignity. And he believed with a passion in the freedom of all things. It is indeed strange that here, upon this sprawling continent we so proudly call the birthplace of freedom, there should stand no great memorial to that first citizen of liberty . . . The American Indian.

—JACQUES LESSTRANG

THE MEMORIAL TO THE AMERICAN INDIAN

. . . First ground has been broken with an access road to the site of the nine million dollar Memorial to the American Indian on a section of land acquired by the Memorial Foundation of Ann Arbor, Michigan, in one of the beauty spots of the Red Rocks six miles east of Gallup, New Mexico.

The Memorial museum and library will serve as a permanent repository for things Indian, where not only scientists but historians, artists, craftsmen, architects, authors, illustrators and others may come to delve into the Indian past or present.

If you wish more information on the achievement of this magnificent effort, write to the American Indian Foundation Memorial, 309 South State Street, Ann Arbor, Michigan, or Indian Capitol Memorial Commission, P. O. Box 1029, The Hogan, Gallup, New Mexico.

THE SILENT CAMP

The night is calm.
A breeze whispers in the lofty pines
As they sweep the clouds in a soft rhythm.
A dainty flame dances over a stage of embers
And the shadows dart mysteriously from tree to tree.
A lonely coyote creeps up and scents the air
And, slinking away, chants a call of the wild.
An Indian lies propped on an elbow:
Lazy puffs of smoke from his fire
Weave a crazy paisley in the night air.
Nearby his horse neighs,
The moon dodges in and out of the floating clouds.
The day is done—Wa-Kon-Tah is near.

> —From Wayne Replogle's YELLOWSTONE'S BANNOCK
> TRAILS, with permission of The Yellowstone Li-
> brary & Museum Association, Yellowstone Park,
> Wyoming

"THE DAY ENDS IN BEAUTY"

APPENDIX

SOME PRINCIPAL INDIAN TRIBES

NORTHEAST

Algonquin
Cayuga
Chippewa
Delaware
Erie
Forest
Huron
Iroquois
Kickapoo
Mohican
Massachusetts
Menomini
Micmac
Mohawk

Nanticoke
Narraganset
Ojibway
Oneida
Onondago
Penobscot
Peoria
Sauk-Fox
Seneca
Susquehanna
Tuscarora
Winnebago
Wyandot

SOUTHEAST

Cherokee
Chickahominy
Chickasaw
Choctaw
Natchez

Powhatan
Seminole
Shawnee
Tuscarora
Waco

THE PLAINS AND PLATEAUS

Apache
Arapaho
Assinoboine
Bannock
Blackfoot
Cayuse
Cheyenne
Comanche
Cree
Crow
Dakota
Flathead
Hidatsa
Iowa
Kansas
Kiowa

Mandan
Nez Perce
Ojibway
Omaha
Osage
Paiute
Pawnee
Shoshoni
Sioux
Thompson
Umatilla
Ute
Wichita
Yakima
Yankton

SOUTHWEST

Acoma
Apache
Cochiti
Hopi
Isleta
Jemez
Jicarilla
Laguna
Mohave
Navaho

Papago
Pima
Pueblo
Taos
Tesuque
Tonto
Yaqui
Yavapai
Yuma
Zuni

CALIFORNIA

Hupa
Kern River
Pomo
Serrano
Shasta

Tolowa
Wappo
Washo
Wiyot
Yurok

NORTHWEST

Bella Bella
Bella Coola
Chehalis
Chinook

Haida
Tillamook
Tlingit
Wasco

INDIAN NAMES

All Indians are given their names in three different ways. The Indian's first name is given to him the day he is born. For instance, suppose he were born at midnight, and a wolf could be heard howling within distance of the tipi. Then the papoose would likely be called "Howling-In-The-Middle-Of-The-Night."

An Indian boy receives his second name when he has grown old enough to play around with other Indian boys. Then his playmates give him a nickname, which might describe what he looks like or something that he does that is different from his friends. Sometimes this nickname might be one that the boy could not be proud of, since Indian boys are quick to pick out some weakness or something funny about each other. Perhaps he might get the name of "Bad Boy," "Bow Legs," or "Running-nose." An Indian boy will keep his second name until he is old enough to go on a hunting trail.

The first time he goes hunting, his brothers watch his carefully, and the way he acts will decide his third name. If he shows signs of being a good hunter, he may receive the name of "Heavy-Shield," "Charging Buffalo," "Good Striker," or "Mountain Chief." But if he makes a poor showing or proves cowardly, he might be given a name such as "Man-Afraid-Of-His-Horse," "Crazy Wolf," "Pounded-The-Head," or "Smoking Woman."

However, if an Indian gets a bad name, he will have the opportunity to improve it on some future expedition or hunting party. A great warrior may have as many as twelve names during his lifetime, all good ones, but he cannot give them to any of his sons, for his sons have to earn their own names.

INDIAN NAMES FOR BOYS

AHOLKING—*Beautiful land*
ANANG—*Star*
ANEKUS—*Squirrel*
ANOKI—*Actor*
APEKATOS—*Antelope*
APELACHI—*A helper*
AYITA—*Worker*
BEBE-JI—*Wild horse*
BEBE-MAK—*Dark horse*
BINSHI—*Bird sharp*
BISANABI—*The silent one*
BODAWAY—*(He) makes fire*
CHABAKWED—*Camp cook*
CHILILI—*Snow bird*

CHIMALUS—*Bluebird*
CHISSAKID—*Juggler*
CHITANITIS—*Strong friend*
CHOGAN—*Blackbird*
CHULE—*Pine tree*
GABESHIKED—*Camper*
GAGOIKED—*Fisherman*
GISHIKSHAPIPEK—*Salt sea of the sun*
GITCHI-SAKA—*Big stick*
HATUJA—*Wind*
HUYA—*Fighting eagle*
JISAKA—*Robin*
KA-BA-TO—*Runner*

KAK-I-NO-SIT—*The tall one*
KEEWAY-DIN—*North*
KITCHINODIN—*West*
KODA—*Friend*
KOON—*Snow*
KOUSHEN—*Raven*
LANGUNDOWI—*The peaceful*
LAPAWIN—*The white*
LI-TAH-NI—*Little flame*
MASHKIKI—*Camp doctor*
MINOWAY—*Moving*
MITIGWAKID—*Forester*
NAMID—*Dancer*
NAS-WAW-KEE—*Feathered arrow*
NIBAW—*I stand up*
NINA-BO-JOU—*Sun god*
NODIN—*Wind*
NOKISAN—*Wonder cook*
ON-JIMA—*Strong hand*
OSEHADA—*White cedar*
PANOSSIM—*Water dog or Sea dog*
SA-QUA-SIPI—*River of mystery*
SHAWANI-NODIN—*South*
SHEBOYGO—*Writer*
SHINAKO—*Land of the fir*

SKAJUNA—*Eagle*
SONGAN—*Strong*
TAHESSAKID—*Entertainer*
TA-HOO-TA-NA-KE—*Rabbit*
TENS-KWAH-TA-WAH—*He who sits by the fire*
TILIPE—*Fox*
TONA—*Turkey*
TUMMUNK—*Beaver*
WABANINADIN—*East*
WADJEPI—*Nimble*
WAH-BIT—*Keen eyes*
WAPAGISHEK—*Sun rising*
WAPAGOKHAS—*White owl*
WAPAHAKEY—*White-body*
WAPOOS—*Rabbit*
WASS-WA—*Spearman, or Big spearman*
WAW-BAN-SEE—*Mirror water*
WAWINGES—*Skillful*
WEES-WEES—*Little owl*
WEETOMP—*Friend*
WINAKOLI—*The Swede*
WOWITAN—*Honor*
YUKPA—*Merry*

ADSILA (ad-see'lah)—*Blossom*

AKOMACHI (ah-ko-mah-chee)—*Sweet*

AKSUTAMAKI (ahk-soo-tah'mah-kee)—*Good leader woman*

APELACHI (ah-pay-lah-chee)—*A helper*

APOLSHA (ah-poke'sha)—*Jewel*

AWENHATAGI (ah-weng-hah-tah'gee)—*Wild rose*

AWEOGON (ah-way'oh-gon)—*Nothing but flowers*

AYITA (ah-yi'tah)—*Worker*

CHOGAN (cho'gahn)—*Blackbird*

CHUMANI (choo'mah-nee)—*Dewdrops*

CHOWAT (cho-waht')—*Little girl*

CHANTEYUKAN (chahng-tay'yookahng)—*To have a kind heart*

DEBWEWIN (dabe-weh-win')—*Truth*

ENABANDANG (en'ah-bahn-dahng')—*Dreamer*

GALILAHI (gah-lee'lah-hee)—*Gentle, amiable, attractive*

GANONKWENON (gah-nonk-way'none)—*She is alert*

HOKTUCHI CHUTKI (hoke-too'chichoot'ki)—*Little girl*

IMAKSIDI (ee-mahk-see'dee)—*Lark*

INAWENDIWIN (in'ah-wen-di-win')—*Friendship*

JISKAKA (dji-skah'kah)—*Robin*

KAIYETSCHEAKI (kah-ee-yates-chay'ah-kee)—*Sings in the air*

KANAGWANA (kah'nah-gwah-nah)—*Evening primrose*

KINIKS (kee-neeks')—*Rosebud*

MANAANG-GWAS (mah-nah-ahng-gwahs)—*Butterfly*

MATACAWIAK (mah-tah-kah-wee'ak)—*Pearl*

MIROPAMPI (mee'ro-pahm-pee)—*Buttercup*

MISHANNOCK (mish-an'nock)—*Morning star*

OAWENSA (oh-a-weng'sah)—*Sunflower*

OKSHULBA (oke-shool-bah)—*Honeysuckle*

OKTALONLI (oke-tah-lone-lee)—*Blue-eyed*

OYONGWA (oh-yong'wah)—*Golden rod*

PAJI (pah-jee)—*Yellow hair*

SOYAZHE (so-ya'zhay)—*Little star*

TANYANMANIWIN (tahn-yahn-mah-nee-ween)—*Woman that walks pretty*

TEHYA (tay'hyah)—*Precious*

TSAWYA (tsaw'yah)—*Pretty, bright*

WAHIHI (wah-hee-hee)—*Soft snow*

WAKISHAKA (wah-kee'shah-kah)—*One who never tires*

WASTEWAYAKAPIWIN (wah-stay-wah-yah-kah-pee-ween)—*Woman who is pretty to look at*

WEQUASH (we'quash)—*Swan*

WIKIS (wee-kees')—*Bird*

WIWASTEKA (wee'wah-stay-kah)—*Beautiful woman*

WOAPE (wo'ah-pay)—*Hope*

WOHSUMOE (woh'soo-mo'ay)—*Bright, shining*

WUSKOWHAN (wus-ko'whan)—*Pigeon*

WUTTAUNIN (wut'taw-nin)—*Daughter*

YUKPA (yook-pah)—*Merry*

YUKPA SHAHLI (yook-pay-shah-lee)—*Jolly*

YUSHBONULI (yoosh-bo-noo-lee)—*Curly-headed*

A PARTIAL CALENDAR OF UNITED STATES INDIAN EVENTS, DANCES, CEREMONIALS, PAGEANTS, FAIRS, ETC.

ARIZONA

The Festival at Flagstaff, Arizona, July 4th.

NEW MEXICO

The Inter-Tribal Indian Ceremonial is held at Gallup, New Mexico, in mid-August. Here is staged one of the most impressive folk demonstrations of our country. Ten thousand Indians, representing many tribes, are offered hospitality at the huge encampment. The program that ensues demonstrates Indian skills and talents and presents an impressive display of tribal ceremonies in authentic costumes, ritual dances of various tribes, parades, athletic contests and interpretive exhibits of arts and crafts. Although staged for the high purpose of encouraging and developing pride in their own traditions, the festival draws a large attendance from outside, many spectators returning year after year. For information, write to The Hogan, P.O. Box 1029, Gallup, N. M.

FIXED DATE EVENTS

JANUARY
1. Taos Indian Pueblo stages its New Year's Day Ceremonial with either the Buffalo or the Deer Dance.
6. Installation of new governors in Indian pueblos, with special dances at Taos and San Ildefonso.
23. San Ildefonso has its fiesta, puts on the Buffalo Dance.

FEBRUARY
2. Candlemas Day ceremonial dances in San Felipe, Cochiti, and Santo Domingo Indian pueblos.

MARCH
19. Ceremonial dances at Laguna Pueblo.
Good Friday—Taos (Talpa) Passion Play in the Penitente Chapel.

APRIL
Easter Services on Taos Mesa, and at Glorieta Baptist Assembly.
Easter and three days following—Spring Corn Dances, at Cochiti, San Felipe, Santo Domingo, and various other Indian pueblos.

MAY
1. Fiesta and Spring Corn Dance at San Felipe Pueblo.
3. Corn Dance and ceremonial races at Taos Pueblo.
24. San Juan Pueblo, annual fiesta and ceremonial dances; at Taos and Acoma, Corn Dances.

JULY

2, 3, and 4. Annual fiesta and Devil Dance at Mescalero Apache Reservation.

25 and 26. Taos Pueblo Corn Dance.

26. Santa Ana Pueblo, Indian fiesta and dances.

AUGUST

2nd weekend. Jemez Indian Pueblo, the Old Pecos Dance.

4th weekend. Corn Dance and fiesta at Santo Domingo Pueblo.

MID-AUGUST—GALLUP INTER-TRIBAL INDIAN CEREMONIAL

SEPTEMBER

Santa Fe fiesta, always on Labor Day weekend.

2. Acoma Indian Pueblo, St. Stephen's fiesta, with dances.

6, 7, and 8. San Ildefonso Pueblo, Harvest Dance.

15. Jicarilla Apache Reservation, ceremonial races and dance at Horse and Stone Lakes.

19. Laguna Pueblo, annual fiesta and dances.

28, 29, and 30. San Geronimo fiesta at Taos and Taos Pueblo.

OCTOBER

4. Nambe Indian Pueblo has its fiesta and dances.

NOVEMBER

12. Tesuque and Jemez Pueblos stage their St. James' Day fiesta and Harvest Corn Dances.

DECEMBER

10, 11, and 12. Las Cruces, Pilgrimage by Tortugas Indians.

18 through 31. Illuminated "City of Bethlehem" Christmas panorama, in Climax Canyon near Raton.

24. Ceremonial Dance Day at San Ildefonso Pueblo.

24. Night processions with cedar torches at Taos Pueblo; Midnight Mass is followed by ceremonial dances at San Felipe, Laguna, and Isleta Pueblos.

25. Christmas Dances for three days at Jemez, Santo Domingo, Tesuque, Santa Clara and other pueblos; at Taos Pueblo, the Deer Dance.

26. Turtle Dance at San Juan Pueblo.

31. Deer Dance at Sandia Pueblo.

NORTH CAROLINA

One of three features in the region of the Great Smoky Mountains National Park is the Oconalufter Indian Village, a life-size facsimile tribal ground. Each day men and women in their tribal dress demonstrate their ancient crafts and the visitor can observe the practice of basketry, weaving, beadwork, canoe-making, cooking, pottery, and the manufacture of weapons.

Next door to Oconalufter is a natural hillside setting in the Mountain-side Outdoor Theatre, where the dramatic history of the Cherokee nation is reenacted, presented nightly except Mondays, until September 1st.

The Cherokee Indian Museum, which contains the finest collection of artifacts in the area, some of them ten-thousand years old. The Museum is open to November 1st.

"Horn of the West," staged nightly, except Mondays, in the Daniel Boone Theatre, Boone, N. C., from the end of June until September 1. Sponsored by the Southern Appalachian Historical Association. An outdoor drama that relives the hardship, the humor, and the struggle for survival of our forefathers.

"The Lost Colony," staged nightly, except Mondays, Roanoke Island, Manteo, N. C. America's oldest outdoor drama. A blending of the theater with brilliant music and dancing. End of June through August.

OKLAHOMA

Indian City U.S.A.—2 miles south of Anadarko, Oklahoma, on Federal highway 281 and state highway 8. Indian City is open every day of the year (weather permitting) from 9 a.m. to 7 p.m. Site of the famous "American Indian Exposition," which is held the third week in August.

OREGON

"Happy Canyon," a unique Indian pageant and story of the winning of the West, staged early in September in Pendleton, Oregon, in conjunction with the Pendleton Round-Up.

WYOMING

The "All American Indian Days" is held at Sheridan, Wyoming, in early August.

ADAIR, JOHN
1944. *The Navaho and Pueblo Silversmiths.* University of Oklahoma Press, Norman. (A good description of silversmithing, its history, and design. Well illustrated.)
AMERICAN INDIAN CRAFTS (Free Catalogue). Plume Trading & Sales Co., Inc., P.O. Box 585, Monroe, New York.
AMSDEN, CHARLES
1934. *Navaho Weaving,* 261 pp. Santa Ana, Calif.
APPLETON, LEROY
1950. *Indian Art of the Americas.* Chas. Scribner's Sons. (A good many illustrations in color.)
BLEEKER, SONIA
The Golden Play Book of Indian Stamps. Simon and Schuster, New York.
BOY SCOUT INDIAN LORE (Merit Badge Series)
May be purchased from any store handling Scout supplies.
BUREAU OF AMERICAN ETHNOLOGY
Smithsonian Institution, Washington, D. C.
BUTTREE
The Rhythm of the Red Man, A. S. Barnes & Co., New York City.
CAMP FIRE GIRLS, INC.
Following Indian Trails, Cat. No. D315, Supply Division, 450 Avenue of the Americas, New York City.
DENVER ART MUSEUM
Indian Leaflet Series. May be purchased for about 10 cents each. 1300 Logan St., Denver, Colo. (Excellent text, illustrations, and descriptions of Indian handicrafts.)
FLETCHER, S.
The Big Book of Indians, Grosset and Dunlap, Inc., New York City.
GAINES, R.
1931. *Books on Indian Arts North of Mexico.* (The Exposition of Indian Tribal Arts, Inc., New York, 15 pp.)
GORMAN, MICHAEL
The Real Book About Indians. Garden City Books, Garden City, N. Y.
GRIDLEY, MARION E.
Indians of Yesterday. M. A. Donohue & Co., Chicago and New York.
HOLLING, H. C.
The Book of Indians. The Platt & Munk Co., Inc., New York.
HUNT, W. B.
The Golden Book of Indian Crafts and Lore. Simon & Schuster, New York, N. Y.

INVERARITY, ROBERT BRUCE

1950. *Art of the Northwest Coast Indians.* University of California Press, Berkeley. (279 pp. of illustrations, some in color. Includes a section on totem poles and also has a very extensive bibliography.)

JAEGER, ELLSWORTH

Council Fires. The Macmillan Co., New York City.

MASON, BERNARD S.

1944. *Dances and Stories of the American Indians.* A. S. Barnes, New York. (With descriptions and drawings of dances.)

PARKER, ARTHUR C.

1937. *Indian How Book.* Doubleday, New York.

RAPHAEL, RALPH B.

The Book of American Indians. Fawcett Books, Greenwich, Conn.

SALOMON, JULIAN HARRIS

1928. *The Book of Indian Crafts and Indian Lore.* Harper, New York.

SETON, ERNEST THOMPSON

1916. *The Woodcraft Manual for Girls.* Woodcraft League of America, Garden City, N. Y.

SETON, MRS. JULIA (MOSS)

1938. *The Indian Costume Book.* The Seton Village Press, Santa Fe, N. Mex.

STIRLING, MATTHEW W.

Indians of the Americas. National Geographic Society, Washington, D. C.

TSCHOPIK, HARRY, JR.

Indians of North America. Science Guide No. 136. The American Museum of Natural History.

WISSLER, CLARK

Indian Costumes in the United States. Science Guide No. 63. The American Museum of Natural History, New York City.

WOODWARD, ARTHUR

1938. *A Brief History of Navaho Silversmithing.* Bulletin of the Museum of Northern Arizona. Flagstaff, Arizona. (Good reference for craft students and social studies.)

The following Indian Hand Craft Pamphlets published by the Education Division, U. S. Indian Service, may be purchased from the Printing Department, Haskell Institute, Lawrence, Kans.:

1. *Quill and Beadwork of the Western Sioux,* by Carrie Lyford.
2. *Navaho Native Dyes,* by Stella Young and Nonabah Bryan.
3. *Seneca Splint Basketry,* by Marjorie Lismer.
4. *Ojibwa Crafts,* by Carrie Lyford.
5. *Crafts of the Iroquois,* by Carrie Lyford.
6. *Pueblo Crafts,* by Ruth Underhill.
7. *Spruce Root Basketry of the Alaska Tlingit,* by Frances Paul.
8. *Crafts of the Blackfeet,* by John C. Ewers.

General Leathercraft—Raymond Cherry. McKnight & McKnight Publishing Co., Bloomington, Ill.

The Golden Book of Indian Crafts & Lore—W. Ben Hunt. Simon & Schuster, N. Y.

The Book of Indian Crafts and Indian Lore—J. H. Solomon. Harper & Brothers, N. Y.

Basketry—Boy Scouts of America.

Merit Badges—Boy Scouts of America.

Basket Pioneering—Orange Judd Publishing Co., N. Y.

Arts and Crafts with Inexpensive Materials—Girl Scouts of America, N.Y.

Basketry of the San Carlos Apache—Helen H. Roberts.

Basketry of the Pimo and Papago—Mary Lois Kissell.

Yellowstone's Bannock Indian Trails—Wayne F. Replogle. Yellowstone National Park.

The Book of Arts and Crafts—Ickis and Esh. Association Press, N. Y.

Indian Story and Song—Alice C. Fletcher. Small Maynard & Co., Boston, Mass.

Social Organization & Social Usages of the Indians of the Creek Confederacy—John R. Swanton.

Antiquities of the Upper Verde River and Walnut Creek Valley, Arizona—Jesse Walter Fewkes.

Fremont's First and Second Expeditions (under the title of TINNEAN).

The Book of American Indians—Ralph B. Raphael. Fawcett Book.

Cry of the Thunderbird—Charles Hamilton. The Macmillan Co., New York, N. Y.

The Coast Indians of Southern Alaska & Northern British Columbia—A. P. Niblack.

Totem Poles of the North Pacific Coast—H. I. Smith.

Indians of the Northwest Coast—P. E. Goddard.

Totem Poles, A Recent Native Art of the Northwest Coast of America—C. M. Barbeau.

Monuments in Cedar—E. L. Keithahn.

Kachinas and Kachina Dolls—Denver Art Museum, Denver, Colorado.

Kachina Dolls, The Hopi Indians—Harry C. James. Caxton Printers, Ltd., Caldwell, Idaho.

Types of Indian Masks—Denver Art Museum, Denver, Colorado.

Masks—A. C. Fletcher.

Indians of Yesterday—Marion E. Gridley. M. A. Donohue & Co., Chicago & New York.

Indian Games—Culin. Bureau of American Ethnology Report.

Workaday Life of the Pueblos—Ruth Underhill. Bureau of Indian Affairs.

The Indian Tipi. Its History, Construction, and Use—Reginald and
Gladys Laubin. University of Oklahoma Press.
Costumes of the Plains Indians—Clark Wissler.
American Indian Costumes in the U. S. National Museum—Herbert A.
Krieger.
The Indians of the Southeastern United States—John R. Swanton.

The reader who is interested in a specialized knowledge of the North American Indian should refer to:

Ethnographic Bibliography of North America, by George Peter Murdock, *Yale Anthropological Studies*, Vol. 1, Yale University Press, New Haven, 1941.

The following series and journals contain numerous monographs and articles:

Bulletins and Annual Reports of the Bureau of American Ethnology, Smithsonian Institution, Washington, D. C.

Bulletins and Reports of the United States National Museum, Washington, D. C.

Anthropological Papers of the American Museum of Natural History. New York.

Anthropological Series of the Chicago Natural History Museum. Chicago.

Papers and Memoirs of the Peabody Museum, Harvard University. Cambridge.

Indian Notes and Monographs, Museum of the American Indian, Heye Foundation. New York.

University of California Publications in American Archaeology and Ethnology. Berkeley and Los Angeles.

Yale University Publications in Anthropology. New Haven.

University of Washington Publications in Anthropology. Seattle.

Columbia University Contributions to Anthropology. New York.

The American Anthropologist.

Southwestern Journal of Anthropology.

Journal of American Folklore.

REFERENCES

Indian Leaflet Series, Denver Art Museum, Denver, Colo.
Smithsonian Institution, Washington, D. C.
The Handcrafters, Waupun, Wis.
Tandy Leather Co., Fort Worth, Tex.
American Handcrafts Co., New York, N. Y.
Magnus Craft Materials, New York, N. Y.
Cleveland Crafts Co., Cleveland, Ohio.
S. & S. Leather Co., Inc., Colchester, Conn.
Copper & brass materials—Groundmaster Co., Boulder, Colo.
Plume Trading & Sales Co., Monroe, N. Y.
American Museum of Natural History, New York, N. Y.
Walco Bead Co., New York, N. Y.
X-Acto, Inc., Long Island City, N. Y.

Creative Crafts for Campers—Hammett and Horricks. Association Press, N. Y.

The American Indian and Their Music—Frances Densmore. The Women's Press, N. Y.

United States National Museum, Washington, D. C.

Roy Anderson, Ketchikan, Alaska.

Eukabi Publishers, Old Albuquerque, New Mexico.

Randolph Plastice, Churchtown-Hollowville Rd., Hudson, N. Y. (Plastic masks).

Joy Industries, Los Angeles 19, California (Gourds).

The American Indian As Hunter—John Witthoft. Penna. State Anthropologist.

Pawnee Bill's Indian Trading Post, Pawnee, Okla.

Grey Owl Indian Craft Co., Brooklyn, N. Y.

The Iroquois Long House, Leaflet No. 12. Denver Art Museum.

Bureau of American Ethnology.

J. C. Larson Co., Chicago, Ill. (Leather).

Kit Kraft, Los Angeles, Calif. (Leather).

Russo Handcraft Supplies, Los Angeles, Calif.

O. H. Dugan & Co., Boston, Mass. (Leather).

American Handcrafts Co., Fort Worth, Texas.

Alfred's Hobby House, 2210 W. Lisbon Ave., Milwaukee 5, Wis. (Indian and handcraft supplies).

Chief Blackhawk, Box 564, Kennewick, Wash. (Arrowheads, artifacts, snake skins).

Lone Bear Indian Craft Co., 154 Nassau St., New York 38, N. Y. (Indian craft supplies).

Mangrove Feather Co., Inc., 42 West 38th St., New York 18, N. Y. (Feathers).

SOURCES OF SUPPLY FOR
INDIAN ARTS AND CRAFTS PRODUCTS

An Act of Congress, approved August 27, 1935, created the Indian Arts and Crafts Board under the Department of the Interior, Washington, D. C. Its function is to promote the economic welfare of the Indian tribes through the development of their arts and crafts. Assistance is given in design, organization for production, pricing, maintaining standards, marketing, and publicity.

Each of the organizations listed herein handles its own business transactions. Inquiries regarding prices or information about their products may be obtained direct from each of these groups.

Unfortunately, the market is now being flooded with machine-made imitations of Indian handicrafts, and in some instances craftsmen other than Indians are copying or using Indian designs on their products, thus making it very confusing to the buying public. When the poet Keats wrote "A thing of beauty is a joy forever" he prophetically expressed the lasting appeal that true, authentic Indian craft has to an ever-widening circle of discriminating American people.

And when Elbert Hubbard followed some scores of years later with a statement that there never was a quality product made that someone didn't cheapen and sell at a lower price, the American sage apparently foresaw the time when the flood of imitations would rise to cash in on the market for Indian handiwork with counterfeits that fool an alarming number.

This summarizes the major threat to the continued health of an industry that not only contributes to the quality of our American culture but also strengthens the economy of talented craftsmen of the Indian race. The Indian Arts and Crafts Board cannot stop the manufacture of such imitations nor is it possible to copyright Indian designs in order to protect the individual Indian craftsman. The Board has the authority, however, to prevent misrepresentation—that is, under the Act of Congress setting up the Board, it may prevent machine-made arts and crafts or hand-made arts and crafts by others than Indians from being advertised, labeled, or sold as authentic Indian hand-made articles.

By buying through the groups listed herein you are assured of obtaining genuine Indian hand-made products of excellent quality. Authentic Indian crafts may also be obtained from traders' stores located on many reservations, from National Park concessions, and from many of the leading gift shops throughout the country.

ALASKA

Alaska Native Arts & Crafts, Juneau, Alaska.
Ivory and wood carvings, baskets, gloves and handbags, mocassins, Indian and Eskimo dolls.

Nome Skin Sewers Cooperative Association, Nome, Alaska.
Fur parkas and mukluks or boots, Eskimo slippers, dolls.

ARIZONA
Hopi Arts & Crafts Guild, Oraibi, Arizona.
Baskets, plaques, silver and turquoise jewelry, pottery, handwoven fabrics, Kachina dolls, paintings.
Papago Indian Arts & Crafts Shop, Papago Tribal Building, Sells, Arizona.
Baskets and plaques.
Navaho Arts & Crafts Guild, Tribal Fair Grounds, Window Rock, Arizona.
Rugs, silver and turquoise jewelry, dolls.

CALIFORNIA
Pomo Indian Women's Club, Route 1, Box 338, Ukiah, California.
Baskets.
District Agent, Hoopa Subagency, Hoopa, California.
Baskets.

DISTRICT OF COLUMBIA
Indian Crafts Shop, Department of the Interior, Washington 25, D.C.
This is a retail shop under the direction of Government Services, Incorporated, Washington, D. C. It is devoted entirely to the sale of authentic Indian arts and crafts which are procured from the Indian guilds and associations listed herein, and also from Indian traders located on many reservations.

FLORIDA
Seminole Crafts Guild, Brighton, Florida.
Patchwork skirts, aprons and handbags; dolls; baskets.

MISSISSIPPI
Choctaw Indian Agency, Philadelphia, Mississippi.
Baskets.

MONTANA
Northern Plains Indians Crafts Association, 804 North 29th Street, Billings, Montana.
Quill and beadwork on buckskin; dolls; moccasins; hand-loomed bedspreads, draperies, and luncheon sets; buckskin jackets and gloves; beaded ornaments and jewelry; purses, handbags; rawhide boxes and baskets.

NEVADA
Wa-Pai-Shone Craftsmen, Inc., Pyramid Lake Indian Reservation, Nixon, Nevada.
Washo, Shoshone and Paiute handcraft: baskets, dolls, moccasins, baby cradleboards, wood carving, jackets, gloves.

NEW MEXICO

Arts & Crafts Department, Santa Fe Indian School, Santa Fe, New Mexico.

Pottery, silver and turquoise jewelry, handwoven luncheon sets, wood carvings, paintings, handbags, drums, handwoven belts, Kachina dolls.

NORTH CAROLINA

Qualla Indian Arts & Crafts Association, Cherokee, North Carolina.

Baskets; handwoven linen towels, table mats and napkins; rugs; handbags; wood carvings; metal crafts; dolls.

NORTH DAKOTA

Turtle Mountain Indian Arts & Crafts Association, Belcourt, North Dakota.

Beadwork; baskets; handwoven scarfs, shawls and baby blankets; finger-weave belts.

OKLAHOMA

Southern Plains Exhibit & Craft Center, Box 447, Anadarko, Oklahoma.

Beadwork; suede jackets, handbags and belts; moccasins; dolls.

Sequoyah Indian Weavers Association, Tahlequah, Oklahoma.

Handwoven woolen yard goods, blankets, scarfs, bedspreads, neckties.

SOUTH DAKOTA

Pine Ridge Indian Arts & Crafts Shop, Pine Ridge, South Dakota.

Bead and quill work on buckskin; pottery; handwoven draperies, scarfs, stoles, shawls, luncheon sets, and baby blankets.

Rosebud Indian Arts & Crafts Shop, Rosebud, South Dakota.

Bead and quill work on buckskin; handwoven scarfs, shawls and baby blankets; linen towels and luncheon sets with petit-point embroidery in Sioux Indian designs.

Sioux Indian Arts & Crafts Shop & Museum, St. Joe & West Boulevard, Rapid City, South Dakota.

This is a retail shop handling the arts and crafts work from North and South Dakota.

WYOMING

Shoshone Indian Craft Shop, Wind River Indian Agency, Fort Washakie, Wyoming.

Beadwork; buckskin work; handwoven draperies; dolls.

Indian Trading Posts
(*Indian handcraft materials and kits*)

Plume Trading and Sales Co., Inc., P.O. Box 585, Monroe, New York.
Grey Owl Indian Craft Co., 4518 7th Ave., Brooklyn, 20, N. Y.
Pawnee Bill's Indian Trading Post, Pawnee, Oklahoma.

Fairchild Woodcraft, 6036 Hazelhurst Pl., N. Hollywood, Calif. (Indian costume kits)

"How to Make Indian Arrowheads." Booklet and kit prepared in the interest of collectors of Indian artifacts so that they may experience the trials and tribulations encountered by the Indians as they made their weapons and tools. Lobo Guild, P.O. Box 144, Carlsbad, N. M.

Birchcraft, Box 590, Scottville, Mich. Catalogue.

Indian Journals, Magazines, and Associations

Indian Council Fire, 30 W. Washington St., Chicago 2, Ill. Founder of the Annual Indian Achievement Award.

Indian Rights Association, 1505 Race St., Philadelphia, Pa. Publish *Indian Truth.*

Indian Association of America, 211 Ward Ave., Staten Island 4, N. Y. Publish *Smoke Signals.*

The Wi-Iyohi, Bulletin of the South Dakota Historical Society, Pierre, S. D.

The Amerindian, American Indian Review, 27 South Wabash Ave., Chicago 3, Ill.

The American Indian Hobbyist, P.O. Box 412, Reseda, Calif.

Indian music recordings: Folkways Records, 117 West 46th St., New York 36, N. Y.

INDEX